The Who

EASY GUITAR SONGBOOK

Cover photo: Getty Images/Michael Putland / Contributor

ISBN: 978-1-5400-3091-7

Visit Hal Leonard Online at
www.halleonard.com

Contact us:
Hal Leonard
7777 West Bluemound Road
Milwaukee, WI 53213
Email: info@halleonard.com

In Europe, contact:
Hal Leonard Europe Limited
42 Wigmore Street
Marylebone, London, W1U 2RN
Email: info@halleonardeurope.com

In Australia, contact:
Hal Leonard Australia Pty. Ltd.
4 Lentara Court
Cheltenham, Victoria, 3192 Australia
Email: info@halleonard.com.au

STRUM AND PICK PATTERNS

This chart contains the suggested strum and pick patterns that are referred to by number at the beginning of each song in this book. The symbols ⊓ and ∨ in the strum patterns refer to down and up strokes, respectively. The letters in the pick patterns indicate which right-hand fingers play which strings.

p = thumb
i = index finger
m = middle finger
a = ring finger

For example; Pick Pattern 2
is played: thumb - index - middle - ring

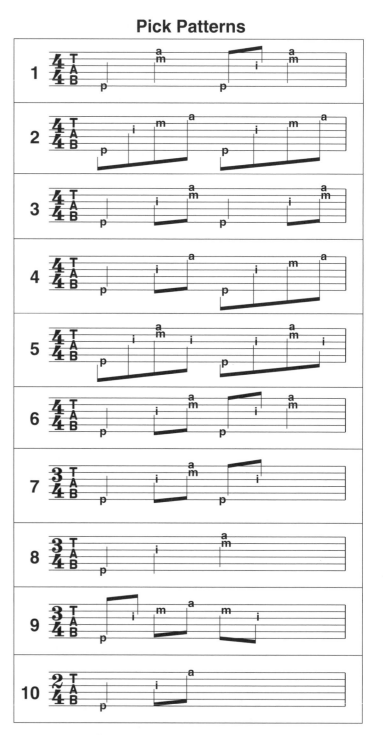

You can use the 3/4 Strum and Pick Patterns in songs written in compound meter (6/8, 9/8, 12/8, etc.).
For example, you can accompany a song in 6/8 by playing the 3/4 pattern twice in each measure.
The 4/4 Strum and Pick Patterns can be used for songs written in cut time (¢) by doubling the note
time values in the patterns. Each pattern would therefore last two measures in cut time.

Baba O'Riley

Words and Music by Peter Townshend

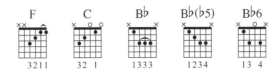

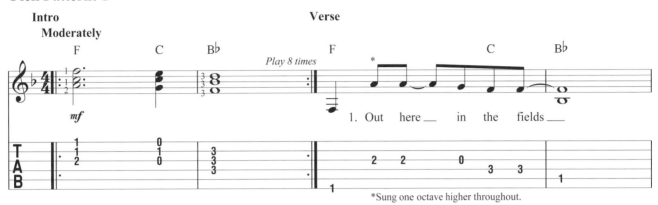

Strum Pattern: 4
Pick Pattern: 1

Sung one octave higher throughout.

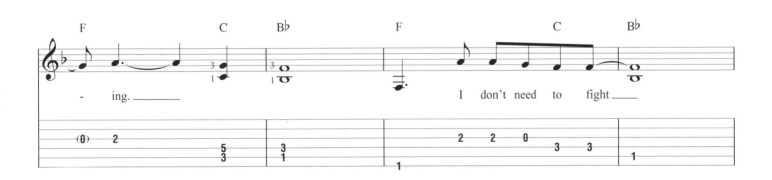

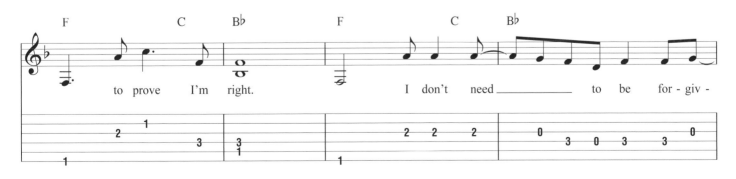

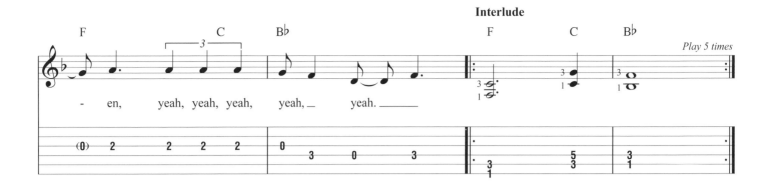

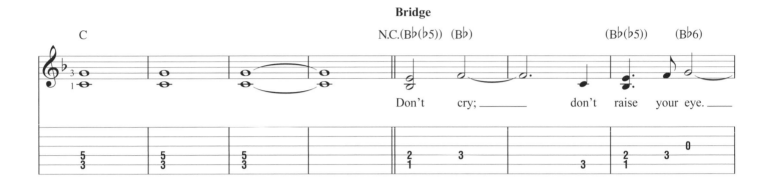

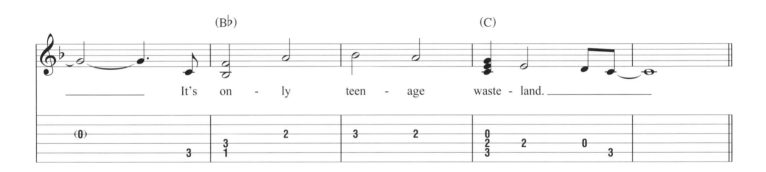

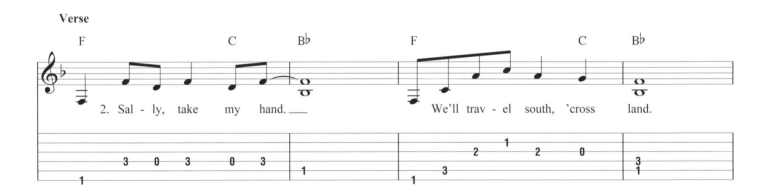

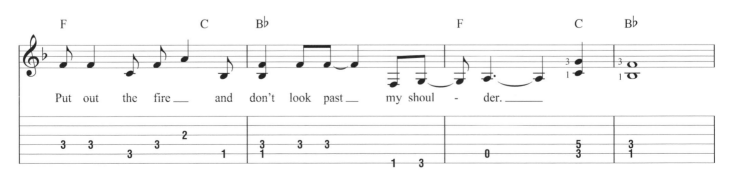

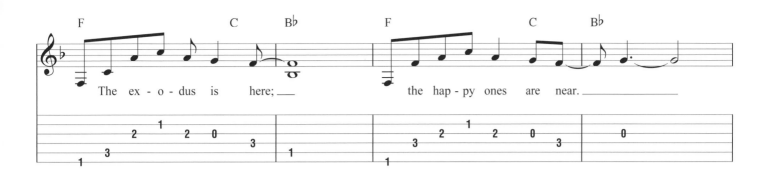

The ex - o - dus is here; ___ the hap - py ones are near. ___

Let's get to - geth - er be - fore we get ___ much old - er. ___

Interlude

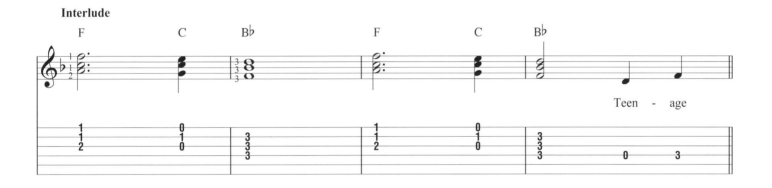

Teen - age

Outro

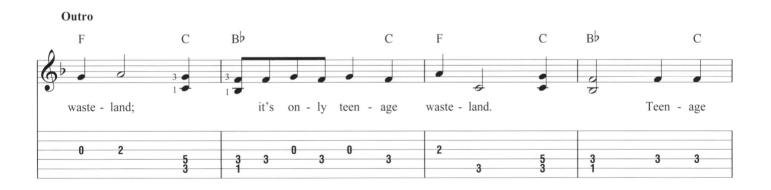

waste - land; it's on - ly teen - age waste - land. Teen - age

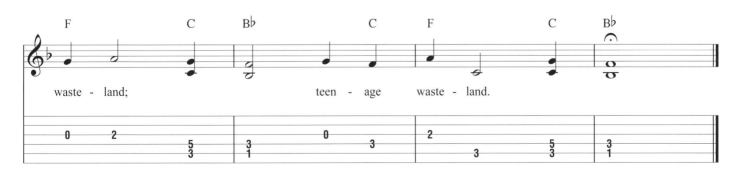

waste - land; teen - age waste - land.

Bargain

Words and Music by Peter Townshend

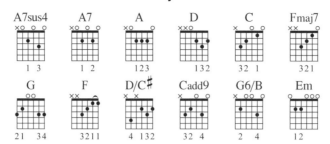

*Capo I

Strum Pattern: 3
Pick Pattern: 3

Intro
Moderately fast

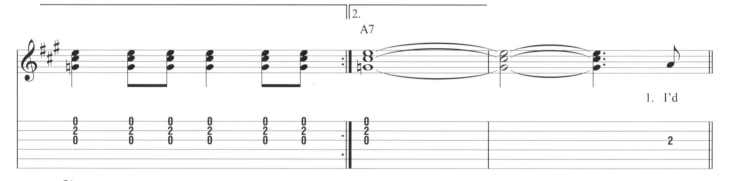

*Optional: To match recording, place capo at 1st fret.

1. I'd

glad - ly lose __ me to find __ you. I'd glad - ly give up all __ I have.
glad - ly lose __ me to find __ you, 'n' glad - ly give up all __ I got.
3. *See additional lyrics*

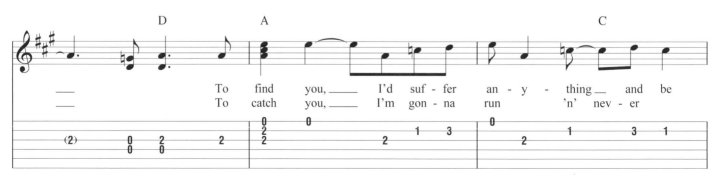

To find you, __ I'd suf - fer an - y - thing __ and be
To catch you, __ I'm gon - na run 'n' nev - er

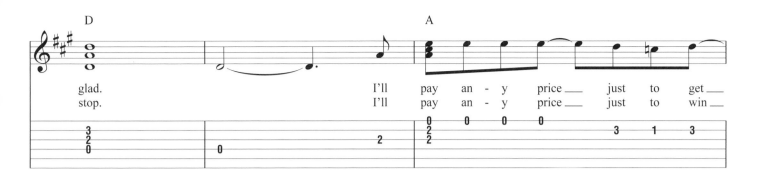

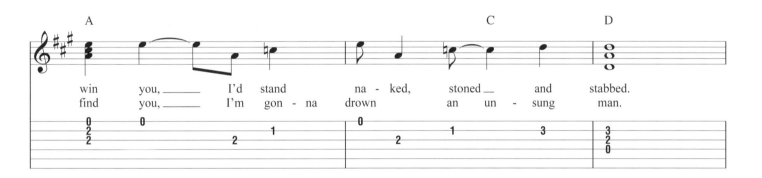

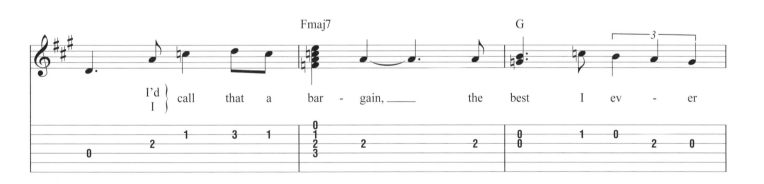

3rd time, To Coda ⊕

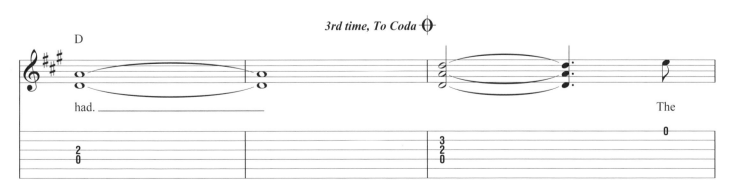

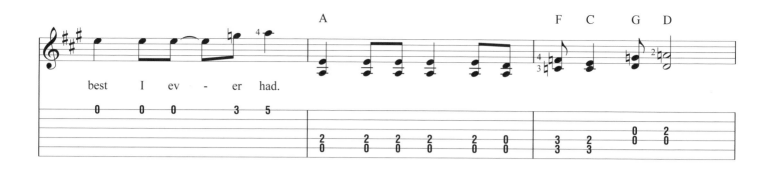

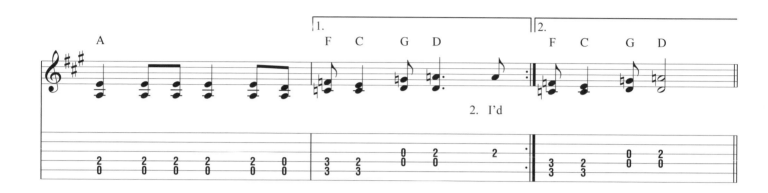

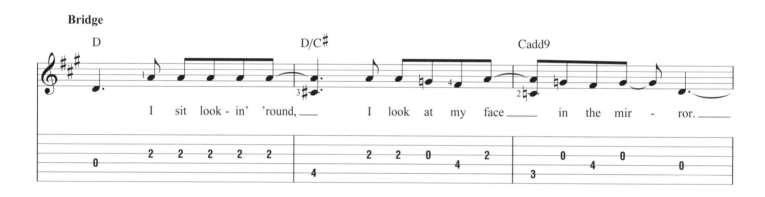

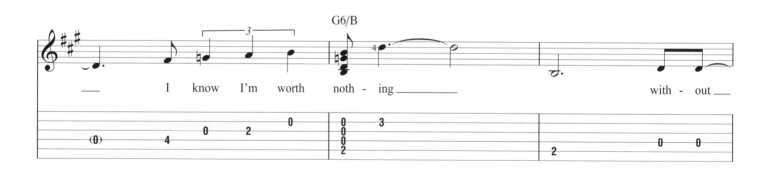

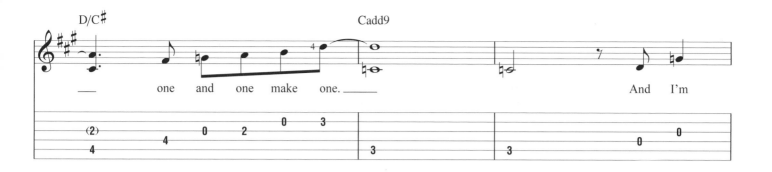

one and one make one. _____ And I'm

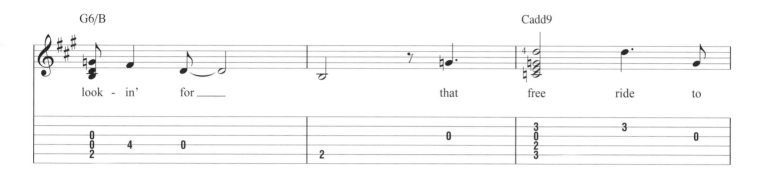

look - in' for _____ that free ride to

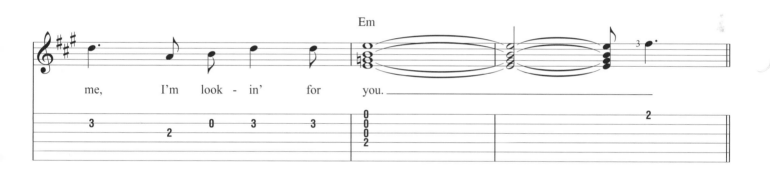

me, I'm look - in' for you. _____

Interlude

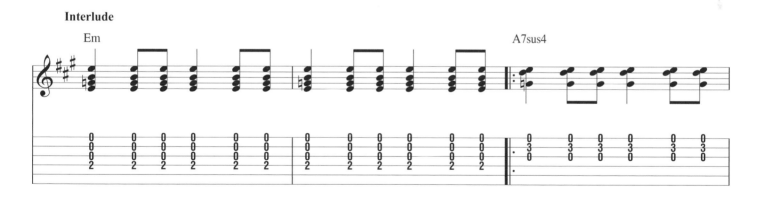

1. - 4.

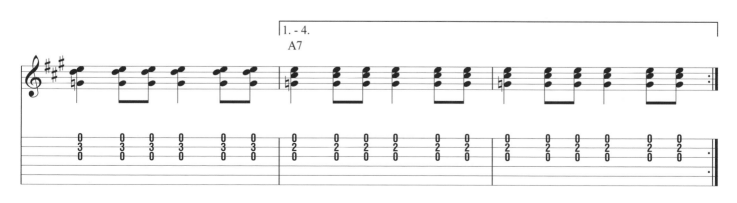

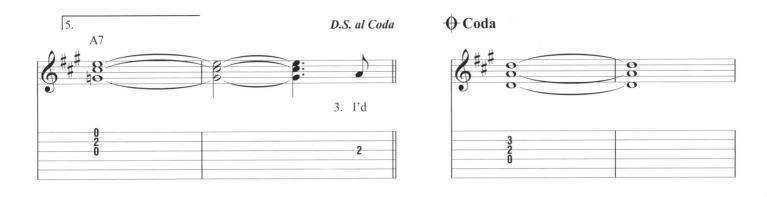

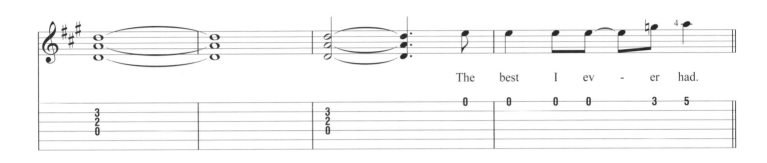

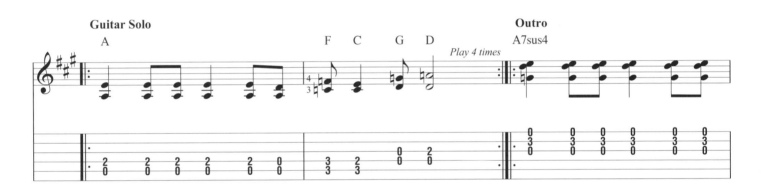

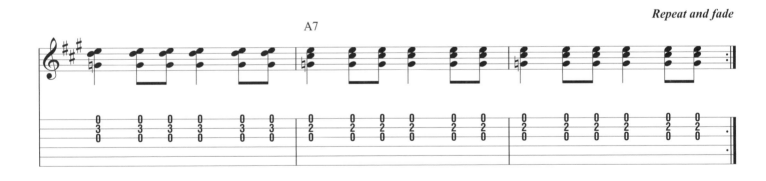

Additional Lyrics

3. I'd gladly lose me to find you.
   Gladly give up all I got.
   To catch you, I'm gonna run and never stop.
   I'll pay any price just to win you,
   Surrender my good life for bad.
   To find you, I'm gonna drown an unsung man.
   I'd call that a bargain, the best I ever had.
   The best I ever had.

I Can See for Miles

Words and Music by Peter Townshend

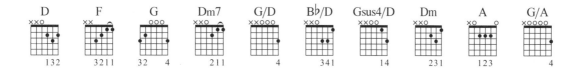

*Capo II

Strum Pattern: 3, 4
Pick Pattern: 3, 5

𝄋 **Verse**
Moderately fast

1. I (4.) know you've de-ceived me. Now here's a sur-prise.

*Optional: To match recording, place capo at 2nd fret.

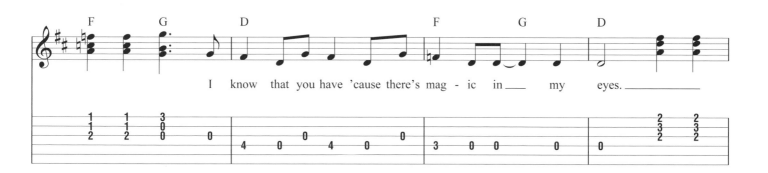

I know that you have 'cause there's mag - ic in ___ my eyes. _____

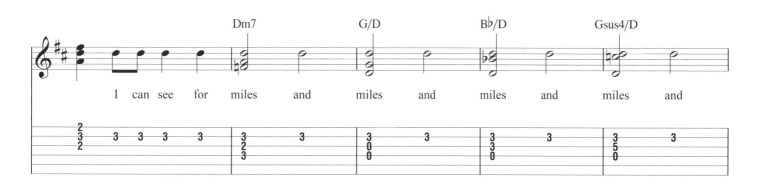

I can see for miles and miles and miles and miles and

11

miles. _____ Oh, yeah. _____

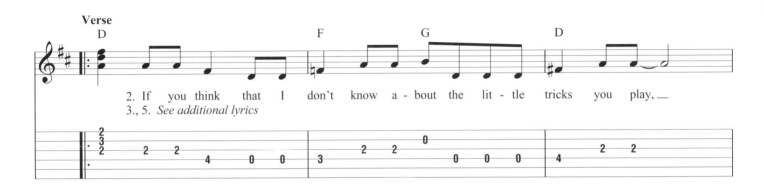

Verse

2. If you think that I don't know a-bout the lit-tle tricks you play, __
3., 5. *See additional lyrics*

and nev-er see you when de-lib-'rate-ly you put things

in my way, __ well, here's a poke at you. __ You're gon-na

choke on it too. __ You're gon-na lose that smile. _ Be-cause all the while, _____ I can see for

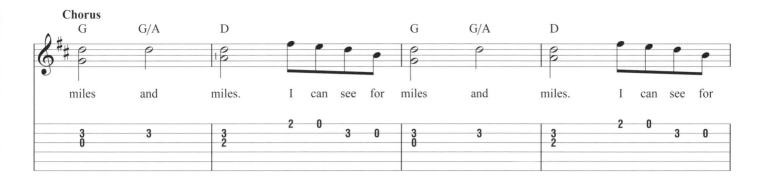

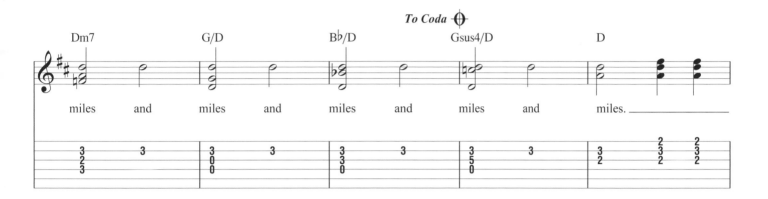

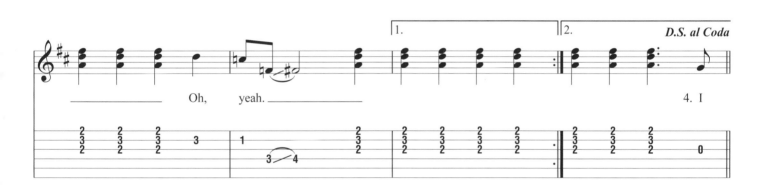

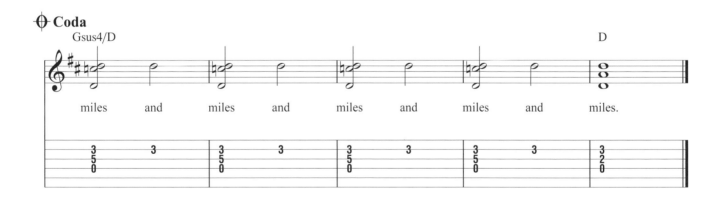

Additional Lyrics

3. You took advantage of my trust in you when I was so far away.
   I saw you holding lots of other guys and now you got the nerve to say
   That you still want me. Well, that's as may be,
   But you gotta stand trial.

5. The Eiffel Tower and the Taj Mahal are mine to see on clear days.
   You thought that I would need a crystal ball to see right through the haze.
   Well, here's a poke at you. You're gonna choke on it too.
   You're gonna lose that smile.

Behind Blue Eyes

Words and Music by Peter Townshend

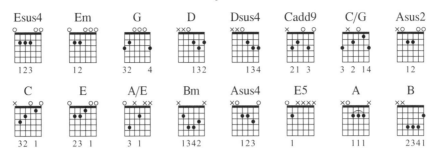

Strum Pattern: 3
Pick Pattern: 2

Intro
Moderately

Verse

1. No - one knows_ what it's like ___ to be the bad man,_ to be the
2. No - one knows_ what it's like ___ to feel these feel - ings_ like I

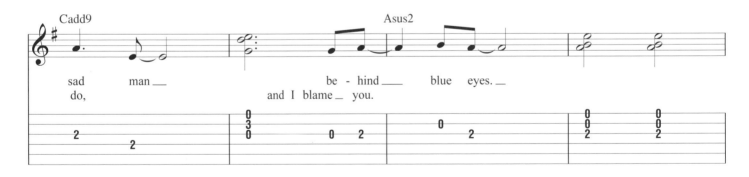

sad man ___ be - hind ___ blue eyes. ___
do, and I blame_ you.

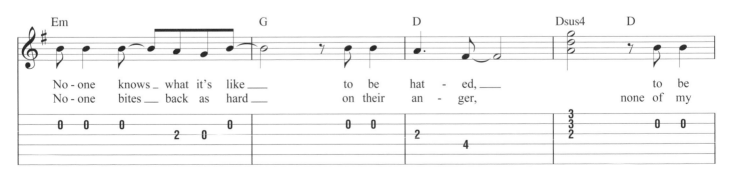

No - one knows_ what it's like ___ to be hat - ed, ___ to be
No - one bites_ back as hard ___ on their an - ger, none of my

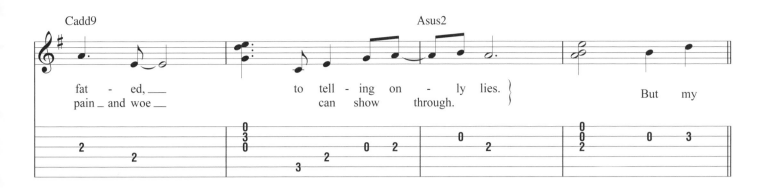

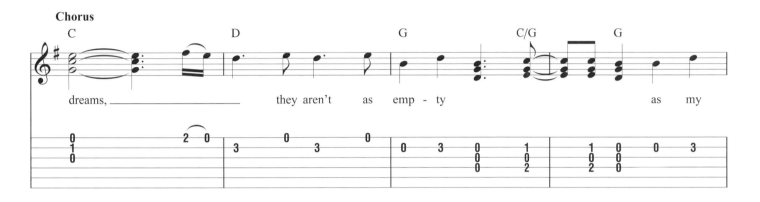

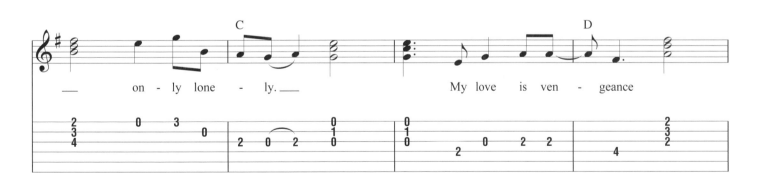

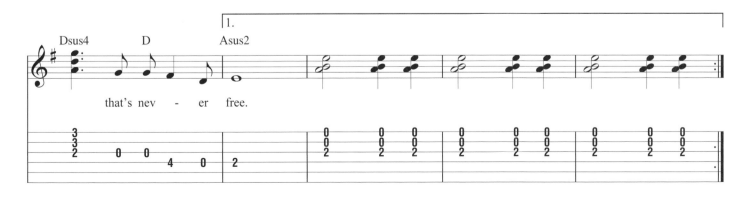

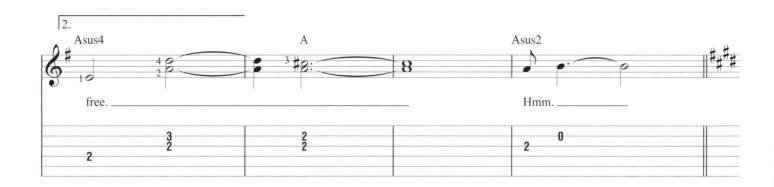

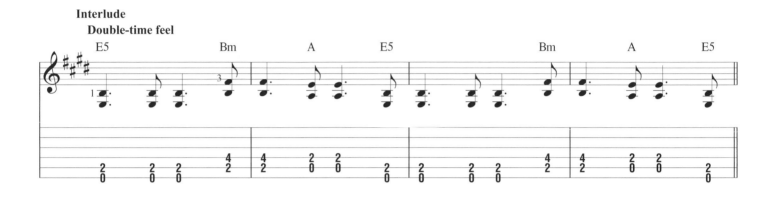

Verse

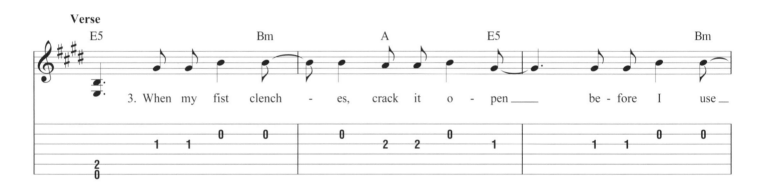

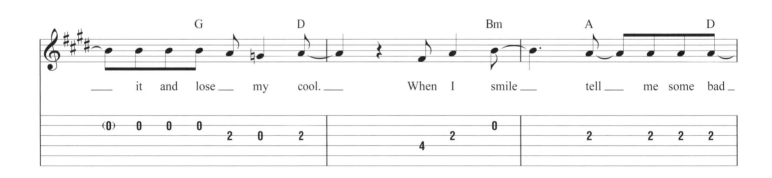

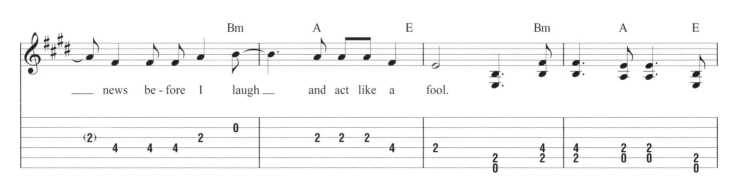

16

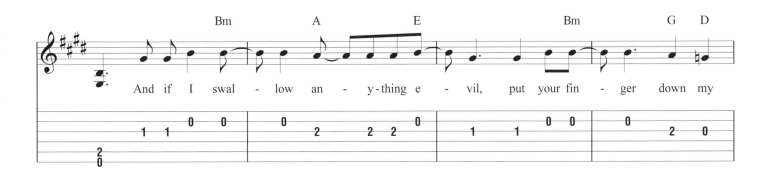

And if I swal - low an - y-thing e - vil, put your fin - ger down my

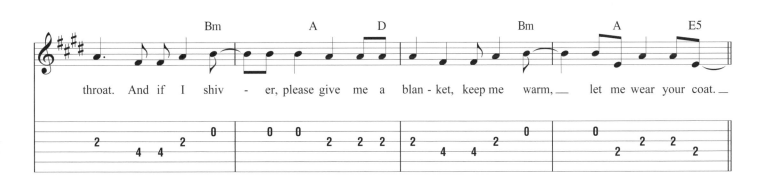

throat. And if I shiv - er, please give me a blan - ket, keep me warm, __ let me wear your coat. __

Interlude

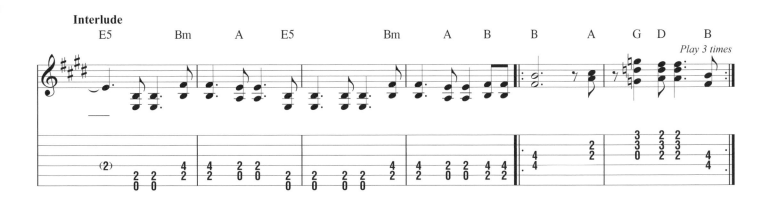

Play 3 times

Outro

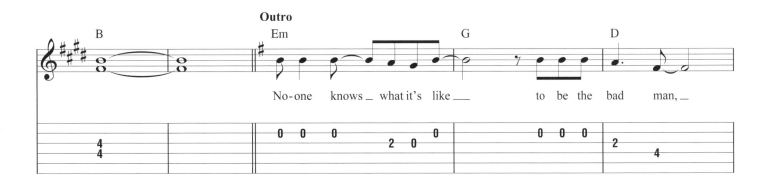

No-one knows __ what it's like __ to be the bad man, __

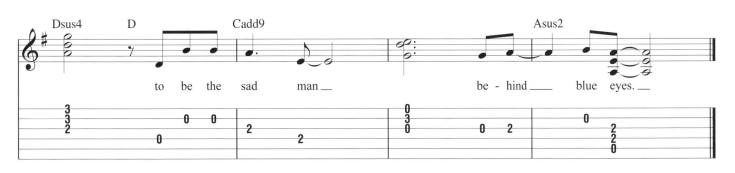

to be the sad man __ be - hind __ blue eyes. __

I Can't Explain

Words and Music by Peter Townshend

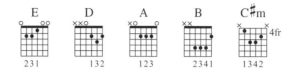

Strum Pattern: 2, 5
Pick Pattern: 1, 6

Intro
Moderately fast

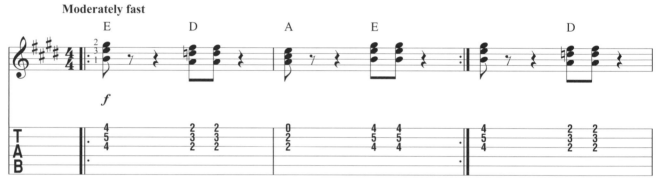

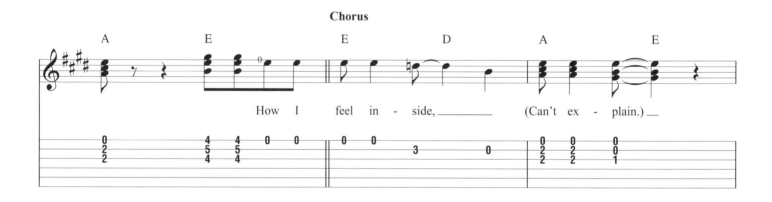

How I feel in - side, _____ (Can't ex - plain.) __

Cer - tain kind... _____ (Can't ex - plain.) __ I feel hot and cold, __

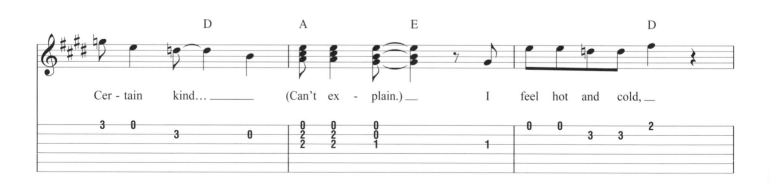

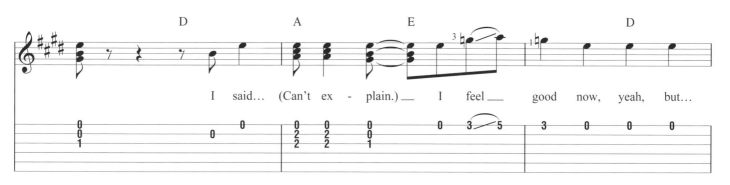

Verse

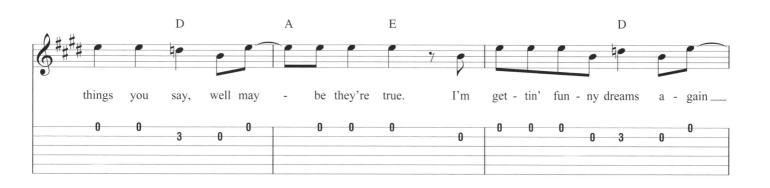

*Let chord ring.

Bridge

Can't ex - plain, __ I think it's love. __ Try to say it to you __ when

To Coda

Chorus

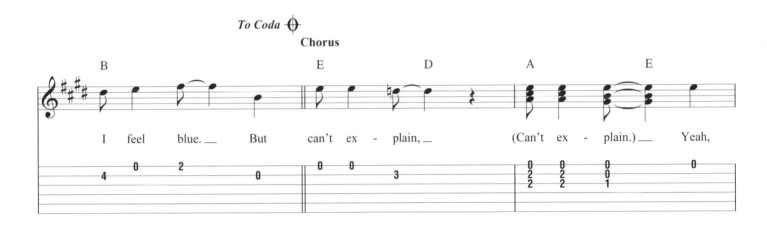

I feel blue. __ But can't ex - plain, __ (Can't ex - plain.) __ Yeah,

Guitar Solo

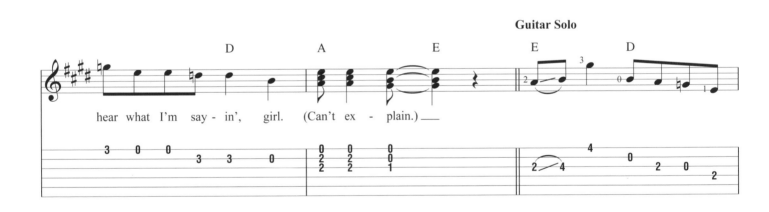

hear what I'm say - in', girl. (Can't ex - plain.) __

D.S. al Coda

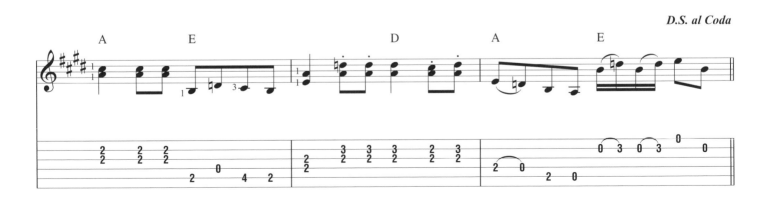

Coda
Chorus

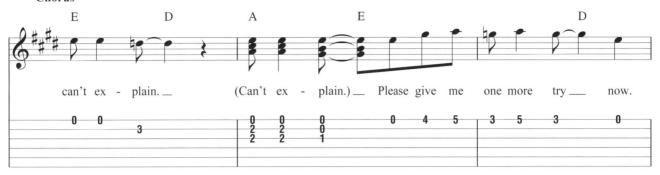

can't ex - plain. ___ (Can't ex - plain.) ___ Please give me one more try ___ now.

Guitar Solo

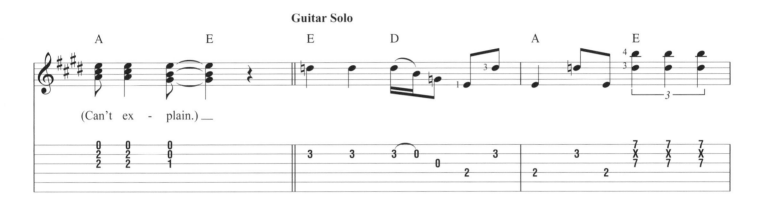

(Can't ex - plain.) ___

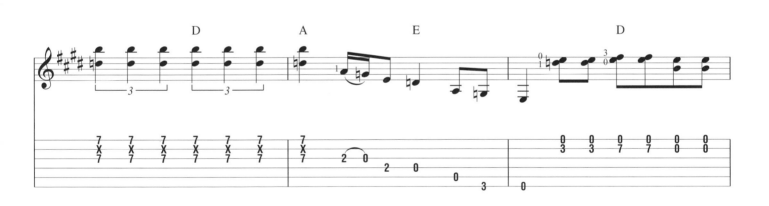

Outro-Chorus

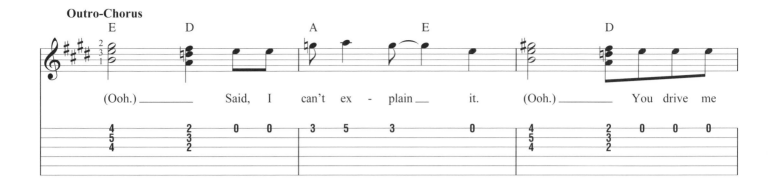

(Ooh.) _____ Said, I can't ex - plain ____ it. (Ooh.) _____ You drive me

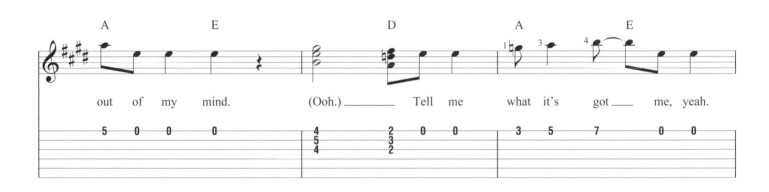

out of my mind. (Ooh.) _____ Tell me what it's got ____ me, yeah.

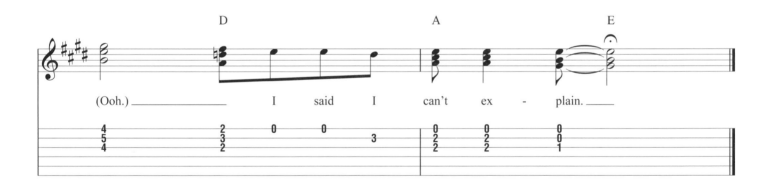

(Ooh.) _____ I said I can't ex - plain. ____

Additional Lyrics

2. Dizzy in the head, and I feel bad.
   The things you said have got me real mad.
   I'm gettin' funny dreams again and again.
   I know what it means, but…

Love, Reign O'er Me

Words and Music by Peter Townshend

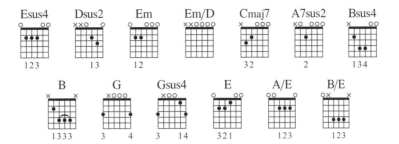

*Tune down 1/2 step:
(low to high) E♭-A♭-D♭-G♭-B♭-E♭

Strum Pattern: 7
Pick Pattern: 9

Intro
Moderately slow, in 2

1. On - ly love   can __ make it rain   the way the
2. *See additional lyrics*

*Optional: To match recording, tune down 1/2 step.

beach __   is kissed by the sea. __   On - ly love

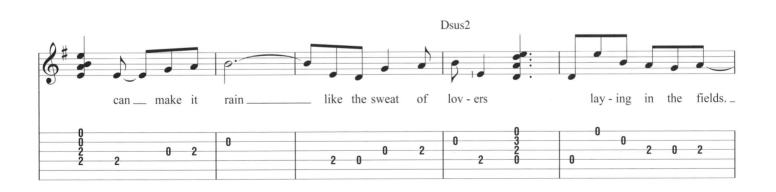

can __ make it rain __ like the sweat of lov - ers   lay - ing in the fields. __

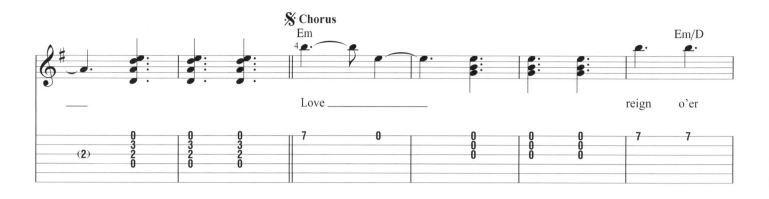

%. **Chorus**

Love _____ reign o'er

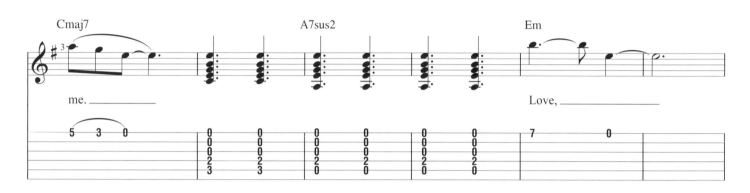

me. _____ Love, _____

reign o'er me, _____ reign o'er _____ me, ___ rain on _____

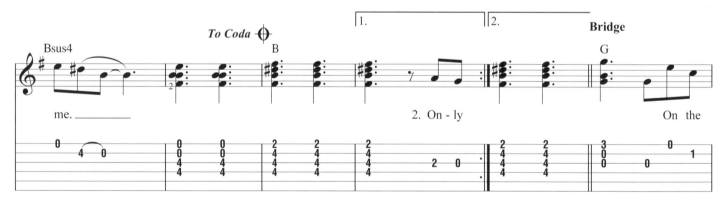

To Coda ⊕

1.   2.   **Bridge**

me. _____   2. On - ly   On the

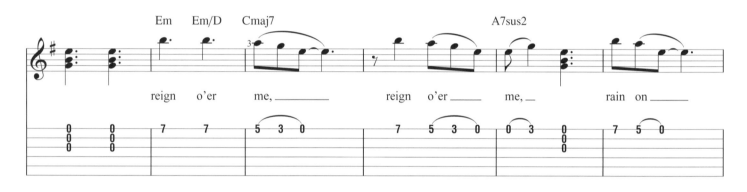

dry and dust - y road,   the nights we spent a - part a - lone,   I need_ to get back home   to

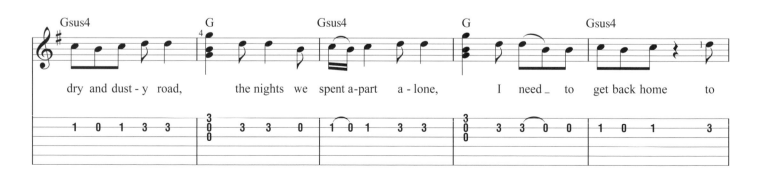

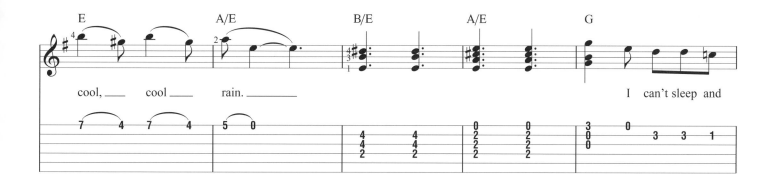

cool, ___ cool ___ rain. ___   I can't sleep and

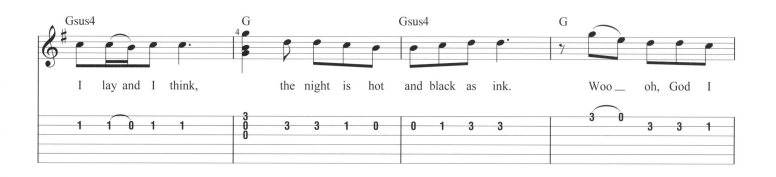

I lay and I think,   the night is hot and black as ink.   Woo ___ oh, God I

D.S. al Coda

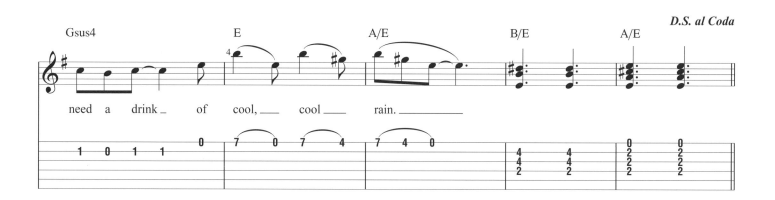

need a drink ___ of cool, ___ cool ___ rain. ___

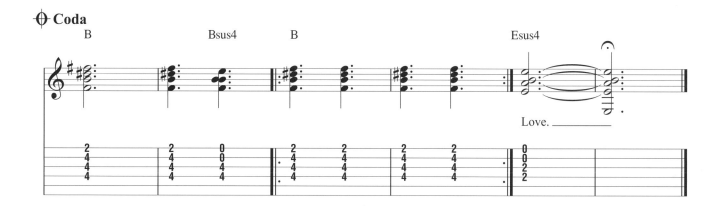

⊕ Coda

Love. ___

Additional Lyrics

2. Only love can bring the rain
That makes you yearn to the sky.
Only love can bring the rain
That falls like tears from on high.

Join Together

Words and Music by Peter Townshend

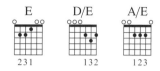

*Capo I

Strum Pattern: 4, 5
Pick Pattern: 3, 6

Intro

Moderately slow, in 2

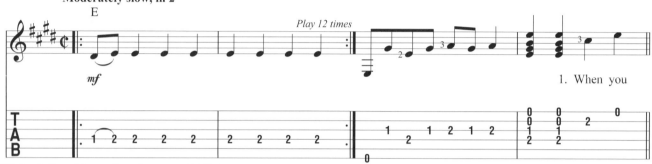

mf

Play 12 times

1. When you

*Optional: To match recording, place capo at 1st fret.

% Verse

E

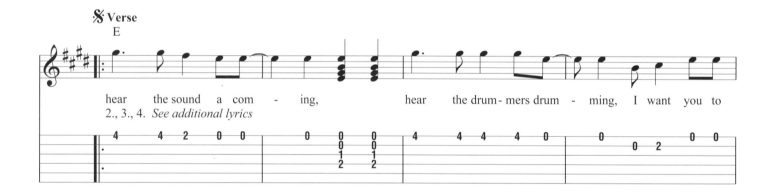

hear   the   sound   a com - ing,   hear   the   drum - mers drum - ming, I want you to

2., 3., 4. *See additional lyrics*

D/E   A/E   E

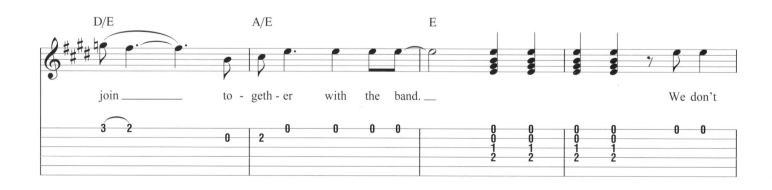

join _____ to - geth - er   with   the   band. __   We don't

move in an - y 'ti - cu - lar di - rec - tions   and we don't make no col - lec - tions.   I want you to

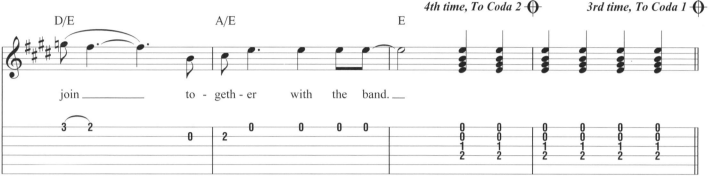

4th time, To Coda 2 ⊕   *3rd time, To Coda 1* ⊕

join _____ to - geth - er   with   the   band. ___

Interlude

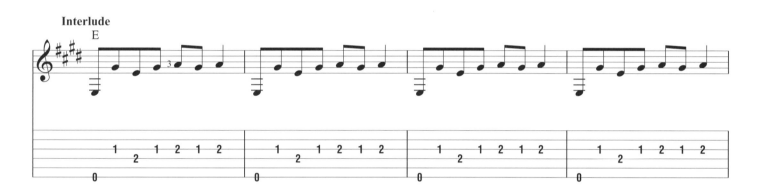

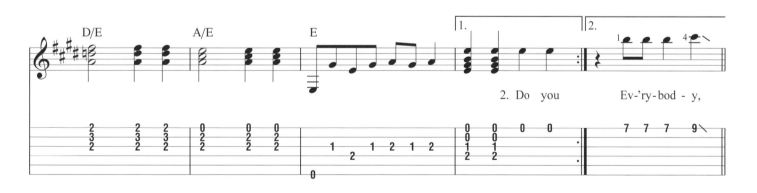

2. Do   you   Ev - 'ry - bod - y,

Chorus

join _____ to - geth - er,   I want you to join _____ to - geth - er.   Well, come on   and

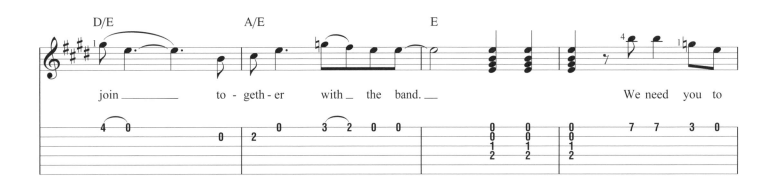

join _____ to - geth - er with _ the band. _ We need you to

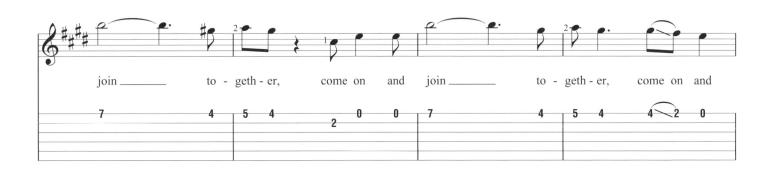

join _____ to - geth - er, come on and join _____ to - geth - er, come on and

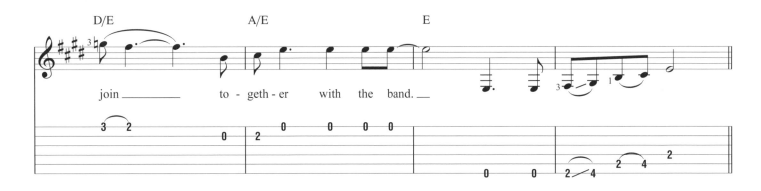

join _____ to - geth - er with the band. _

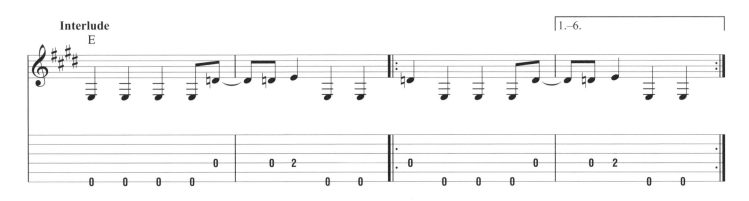

Interlude

1.–6.

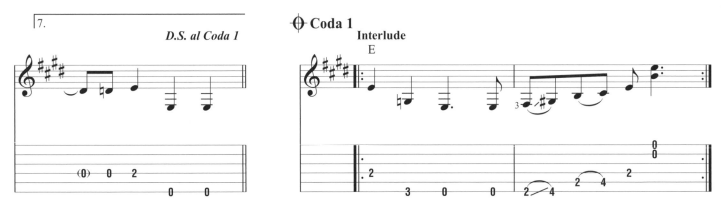

7.

D.S. al Coda 1

Coda 1

Interlude

Coda 2

Chorus
w/ Vocal ad lib.

Hey, hey, hey, hey, hey.   Join _____ to - geth- er,   join _____ to -

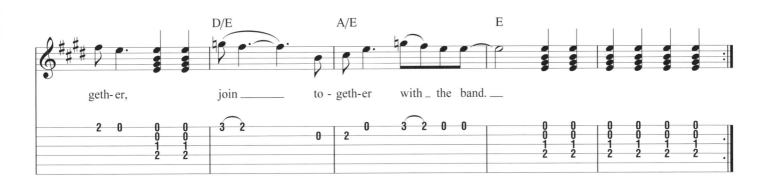

geth- er,   join _____ to - geth-er   with _ the band. __

Outro

Repeat and fade

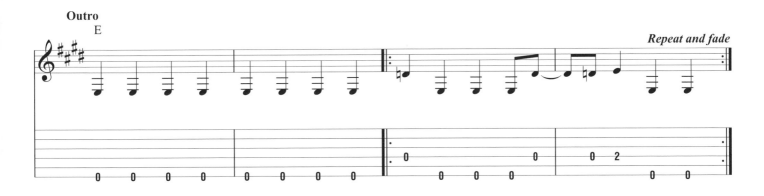

Additional Lyrics

2. Do you really think I care what you read or what you wear?
   I want you to join together with the band.
   There's a million ways to laugh, and everyone's a path.
   Come on and join together with the band.

3. You don't have to pay, and you can follow or lead the way.
   I want you to join together with the band.
   We won't know where we're going, but the season's ripe for knowing.
   I want you to join together with the band.

4. It's the singer, not the song that makes the music move along.
   I want you to join together with the band.
   This is the biggest band you'll find; it's as deep as it is wide.
   Come on and join together with the band.

The Magic Bus

Words and Music by Peter Townshend

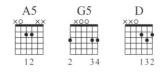

*Tune down 1/2 step:
(low to high) Eb-Ab-Db-Gb-Bb-Eb

Strum Pattern: 3, 4
Pick Pattern: 3, 4

Intro
Very fast

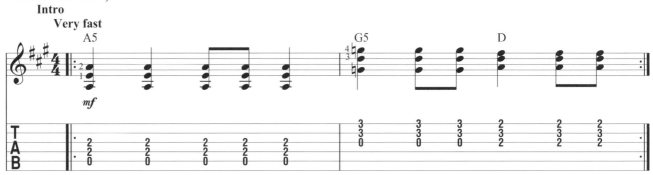

*Optional: To match recording, tune down 1/2 step.

§ **Verse**

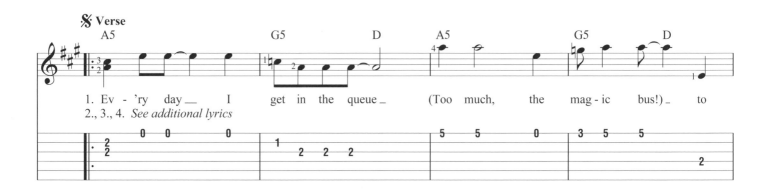

1. Ev - 'ry day ___ I get in the queue ___ (Too much, the mag - ic bus!) ___ to
2., 3., 4. *See additional lyrics*

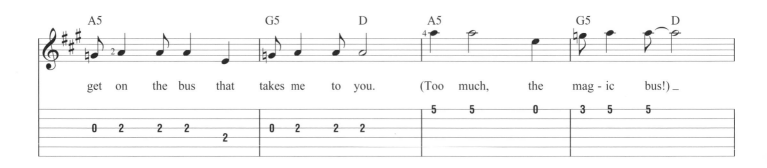

get on the bus that takes me to you. (Too much, the mag - ic bus!) ___

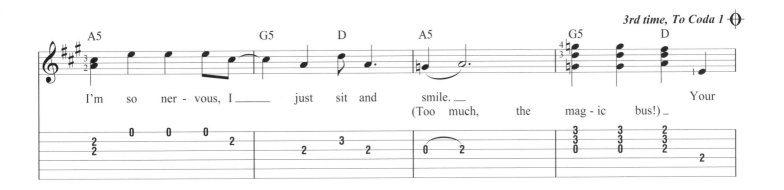

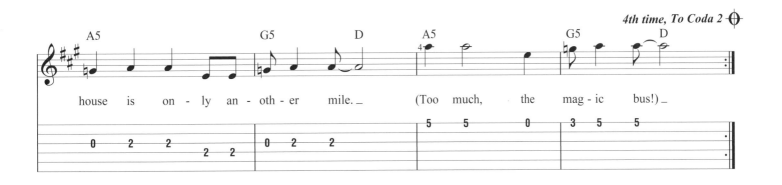

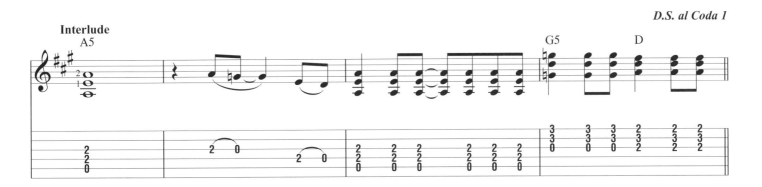

⊕ Coda 1

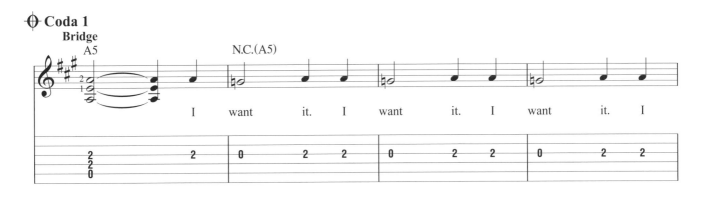

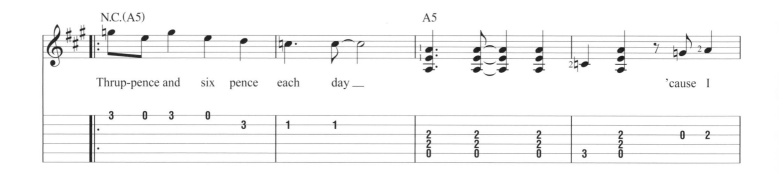

Thrup-pence and six pence each day __ 'cause I

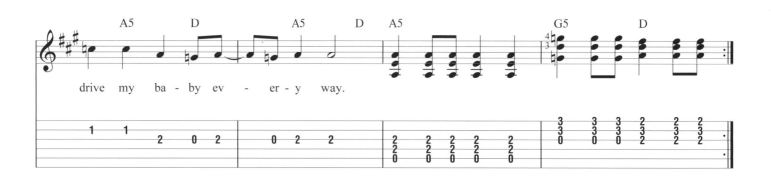

drive my ba - by ev - er - y way.

Chorus
w/ lead voc. ad lib.

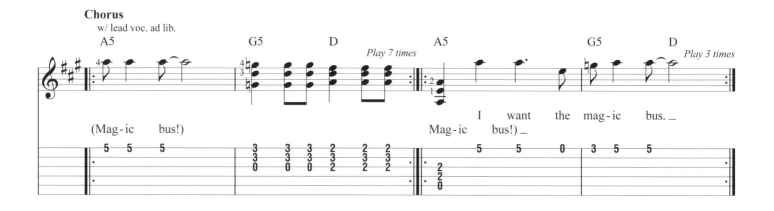

(Mag-ic bus!) Mag-ic bus!) __ I want the mag-ic bus. __

D.S. al Coda 2

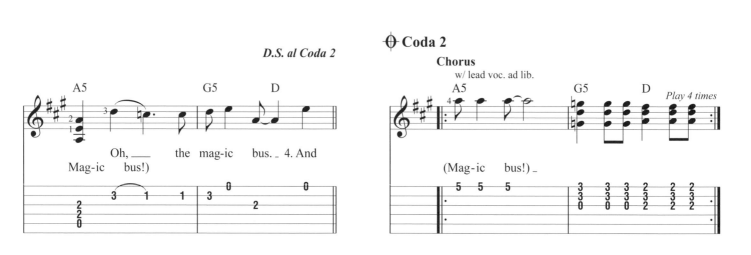

Oh, __ the mag-ic bus. _ 4. And
Mag-ic bus!)

⊕ Coda 2

Chorus
w/ lead voc. ad lib.

(Mag-ic bus!) _

Verse

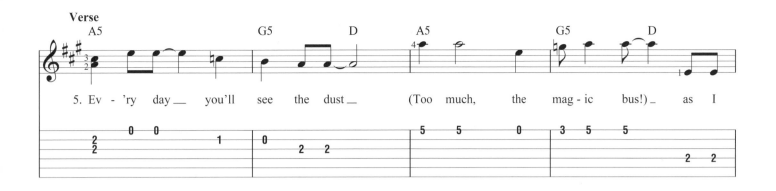

5. Ev - 'ry day — you'll see the dust — (Too much, the mag - ic bus!) — as I

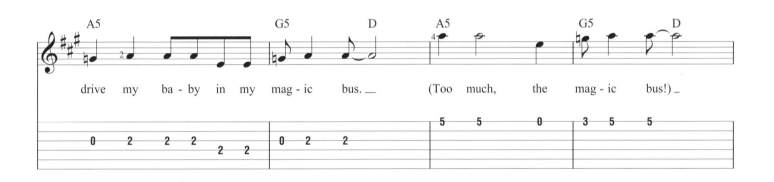

drive my ba - by in my mag - ic bus. — (Too much, the mag - ic bus!) —

Outro-Chorus

Repeat and fade

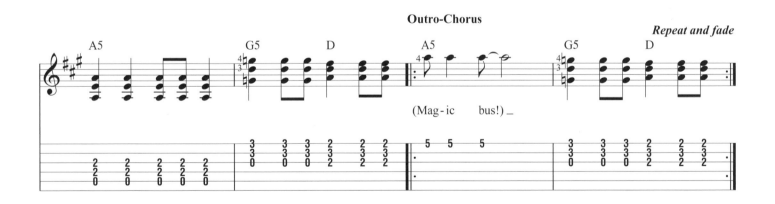

(Mag - ic bus!) —

Additional Lyrics

2. Thank you, driver, for gettin' me here. (Too much, the magic bus!)
   You'll be an inspector, have no fear. (Too much, the magic bus!)
   I don't wanna cause no fuss, (Too much, the magic bus!)
   But can I buy your magic bus? (Too much, the magic bus!)

3. I don't care how much I pay. (Too much, the magic bus!)
   I wanna drive my bus to my baby each day. (Too much, the magic bus!)

4. And now I got my magic bus. (Too much, the magic bus!)
   I said, now I got my magic bus. (Too much, the magic bus!)
   I drive my baby every way. (Too much, the magic bus!)
   Each time I go a different way. (Too much, the magic bus!)

My Generation

Words and Music by Peter Townshend

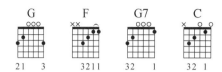

Strum Pattern: 4
Pick Pattern: 5

Verse
Fast Rock

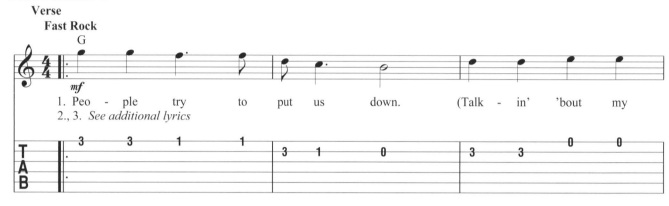

1. Peo - ple try to put us down. (Talk - in' 'bout my
2., 3. *See additional lyrics*

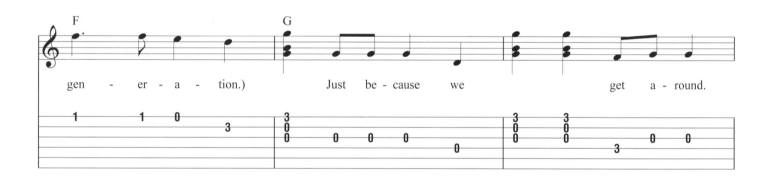

gen - er - a - tion.) Just be - cause we get a - round.

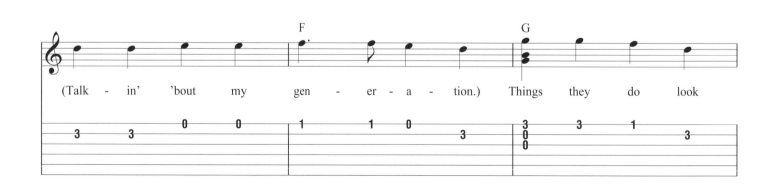

(Talk - in' 'bout my gen - er - a - tion.) Things they do look

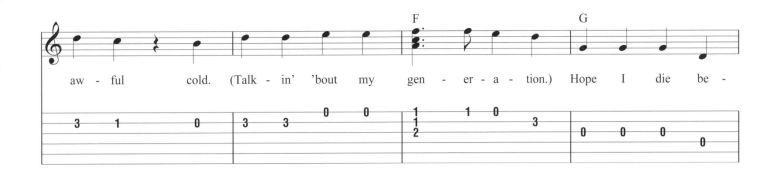

aw - ful   cold. (Talk - in' 'bout my   gen - er - a - tion.) Hope I   die be -

fore I get   old.   This is my   gen - er -

Chorus

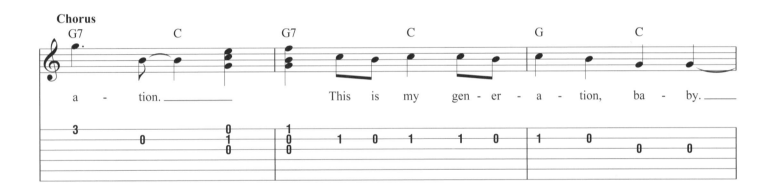

a -   tion. _____ This is my   gen - er - a - tion, ba - by. _____

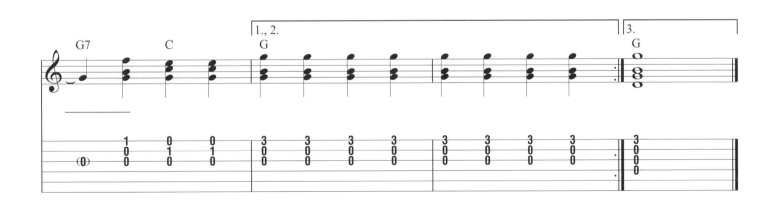

Additional Lyrics

2., 3. Why don't you all fade away? (Talkin' 'bout my generation.)
Don't try to dig what we all say. (Talkin' 'bout my generation.)
I'm not tryin' to cause a big sensation. (Talkin' 'bout my generation.)
I'm just talkin' 'bout my generation. (Talkin' 'bout my generation.)

Pinball Wizard

Words and Music by Peter Townshend

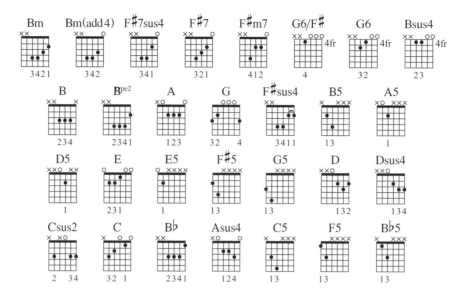

Strum Pattern: 2
Pick Pattern: 2

Intro

Moderately

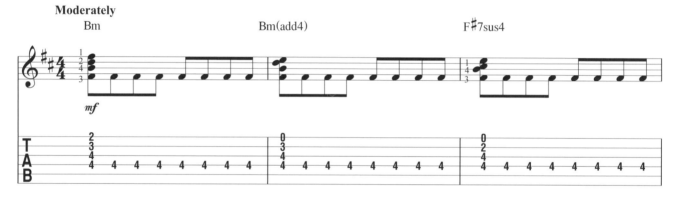

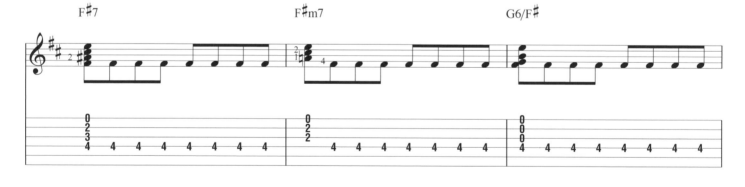

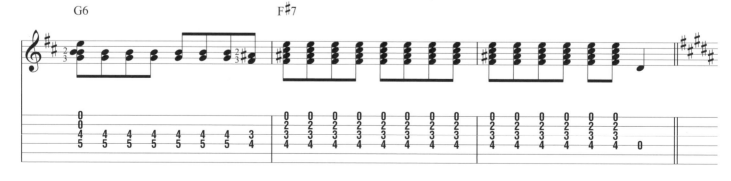

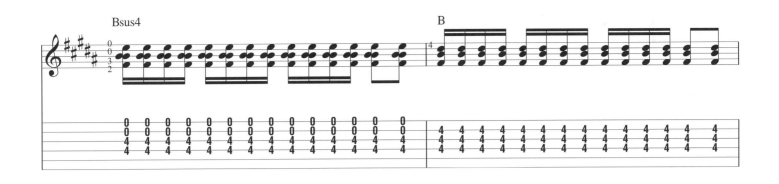

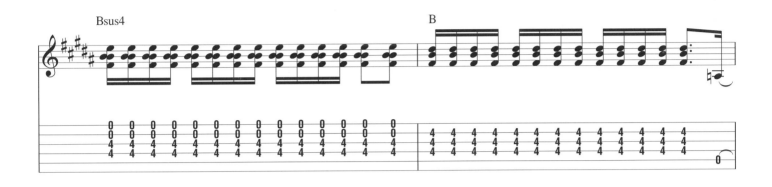

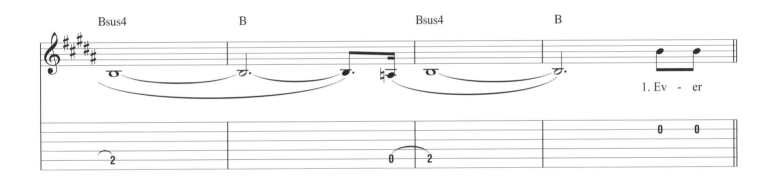

Verse

since I was a young boy, I've played the sil - ver ball. From So - ho down to Bright - on, I
2., 3. See additional lyrics

must have played 'em all. But I ain't seen noth - in' like him in an - y a - muse - ment hall. That

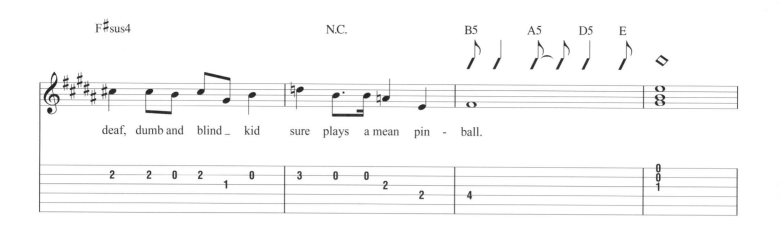

deaf, dumb and blind _ kid sure plays a mean pin - ball.

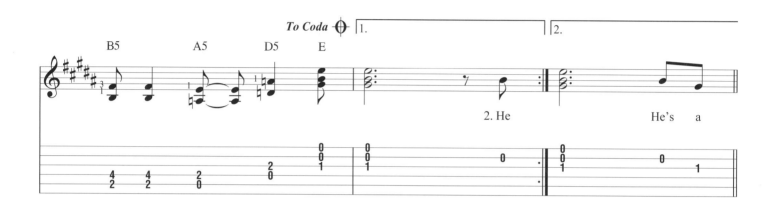

2. He   He's a

Chorus

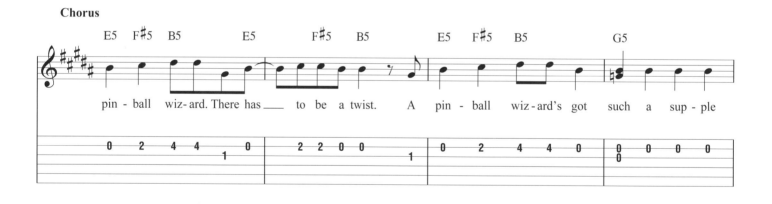

pin - ball wiz-ard. There has ___ to be a twist.   A   pin - ball wiz-ard's got such a sup - ple

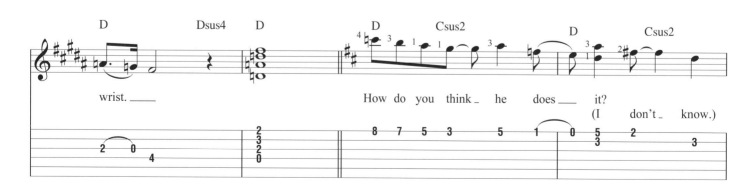

wrist. ___   How do you think _ he does ___ it?
                                    (I don't _ know.)

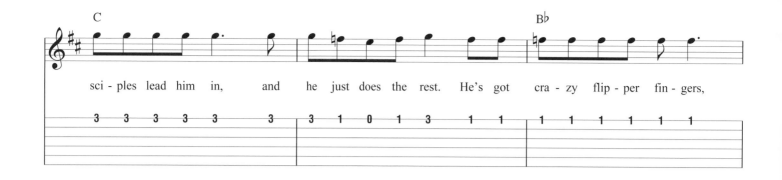

sci - ples lead him in,   and   he just does the rest.   He's got   cra - zy flip - per fin - gers,

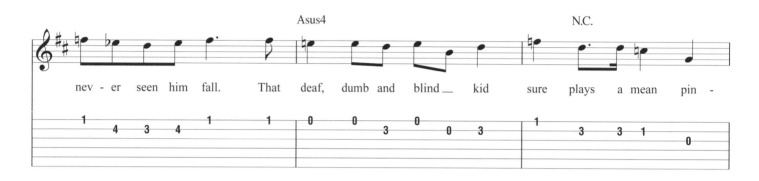

nev - er   seen him fall.   That   deaf,   dumb and   blind __   kid   sure   plays   a   mean   pin -

Outro

Repeat and fade

ball.

Additional Lyrics

2. He stands like a statue, becomes part of the machine.
   Feelin' all the bumpers, always playing clean.
   Plays by intuition, the digit counters fall.
   That deaf, dumb and blind kid sure plays a mean pinball.

3. Ain't go no distractions, can't hear no buzzers and bells.
   Don't see no lights flashin', plays by sense of smell.
   Always gets a replay, never seen him fall.
   That deaf, dumb and blind kid sure plays a mean pinball.

Substitute

Words and Music by Peter Townshend

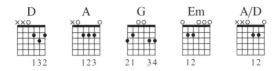

*Strum Pattern: 3
*Pick Pattern: 3

Intro
Moderately

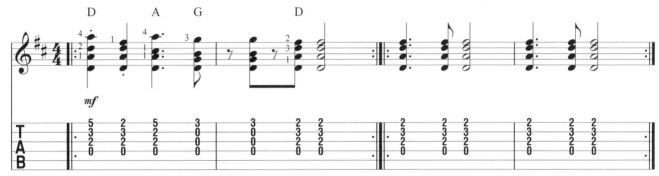

*Use pattern 10 for 2/4 meas.

Verse

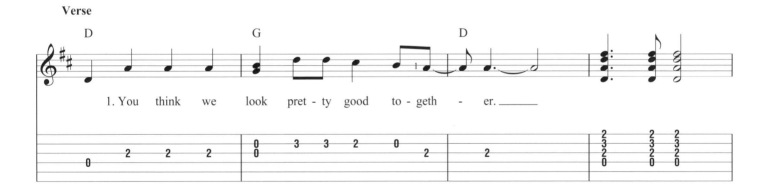

1. You think we look pret-ty good to-geth - er. _____

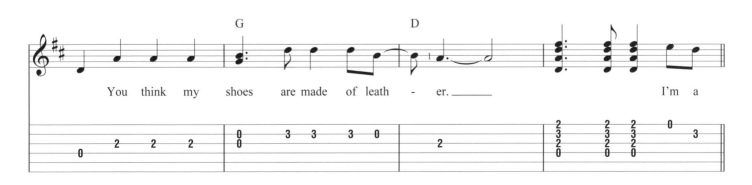

You think my shoes are made of leath - er. _____ I'm a

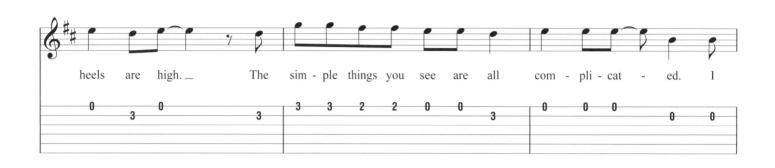

Chorus

To Coda 1 ⊕

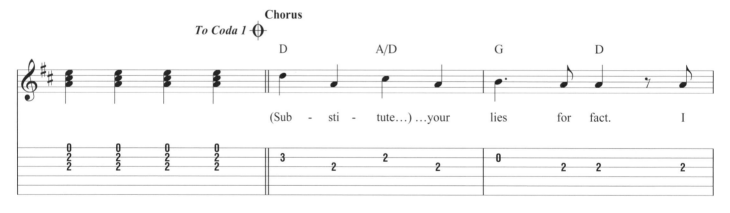

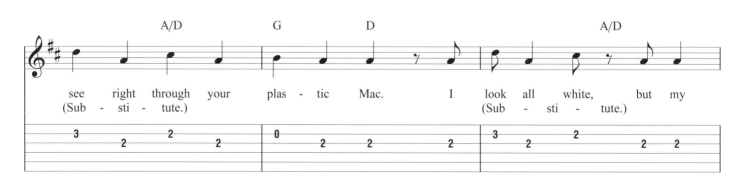

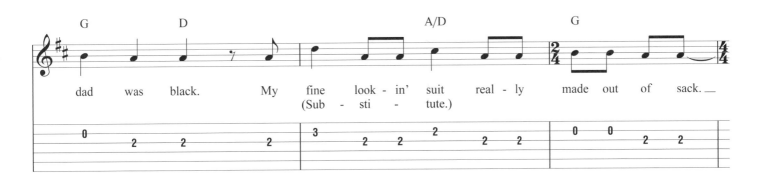

𝄋𝄋 **Verse**

*Let chord ring.

Pre-Chorus

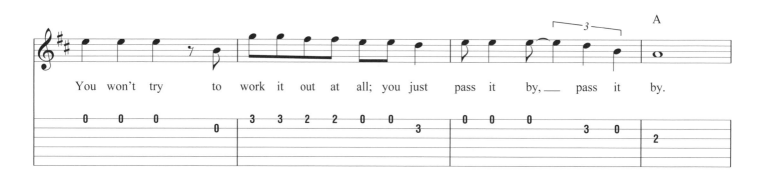

You won't try to work it out at all; you just pass it by, __ pass it by.

Chorus

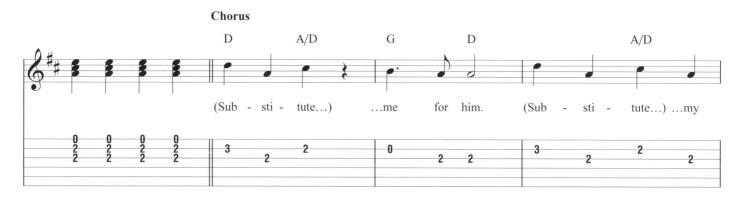

(Sub - sti - tute...) ...me for him. (Sub - sti - tute...) ...my

To Coda 2

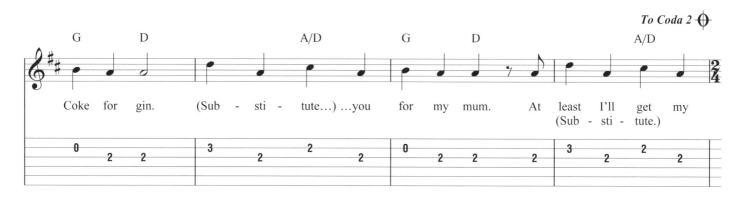

Coke for gin. (Sub - sti - tute...) ...you for my mum. At least I'll get my
(Sub - sti - tute.)

Interlude

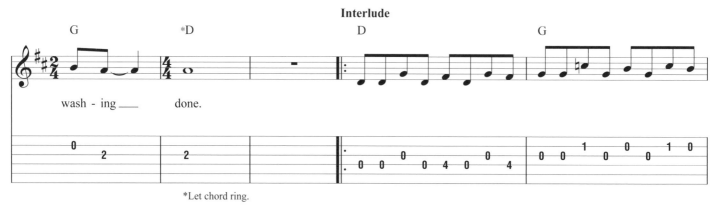

wash - ing __ done.

*Let chord ring.

D.S. al Coda 1

I'm a

The Real Me

Words and Music by Peter Townshend

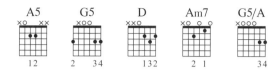

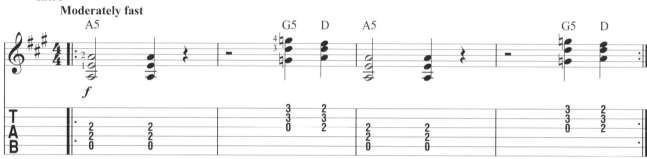

*Capo III

Strum Pattern: 2
Pick Pattern: 4

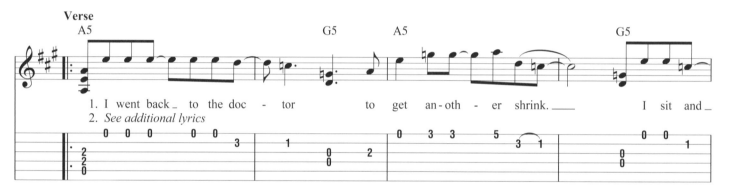

*Optional: To match recording, place capo at 3rd fret.

riv-ers of flow-ing veins. Strange peo-ple who know _ me look-ing from be - hind ev-'ry win-dow pane. _

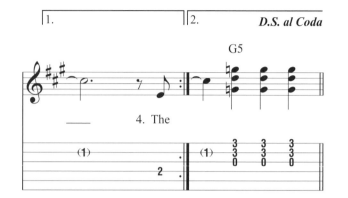

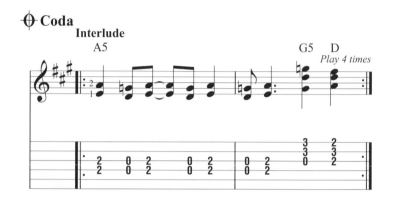

D.S. al Coda

Coda

Interlude

4. The

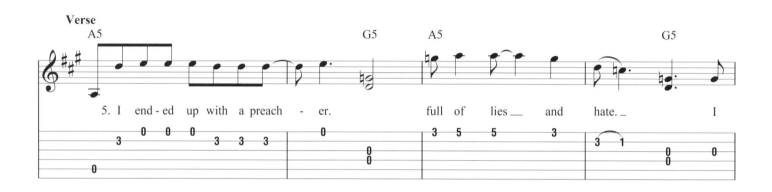

Verse

5. I end-ed up with a preach - er. full of lies _ and hate. _ I

seemed to scare _ him a lit - tle, so he showed me to the gold-en gate. _____

Chorus

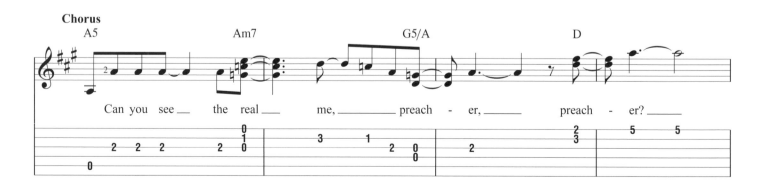

Can you see _ the real _ me, _____ preach - er, _____ preach - er? _____

Additional Lyrics

2. I went back to my mother.
   I said, "I'm cazy, Ma, help me."
   She said, "I know how it feels, son,
   'Cause it runs in the family."

4. The girl I used to love
   Lives in this yellow house.
   Yesterday she passed me by;
   She doesn't want to know me now. Whoa!

Won't Get Fooled Again

Words and Music by Peter Townshend

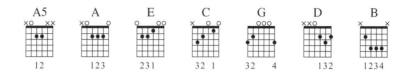

Strum Pattern: 5
Pick Pattern: 1

Intro
Moderately fast

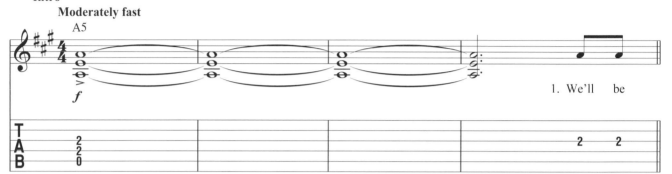

1. We'll be

fight-ing in the streets ___ with our chil-dren at our feet, ___ and the
2., 3. *See additional lyrics*

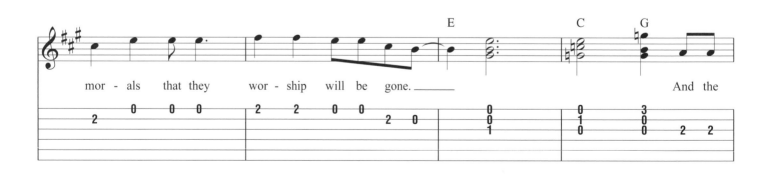

mor-als that they wor-ship will be gone. ___ And the

men who spurred us on ____ sit in judge-ment of all wrong, they de-

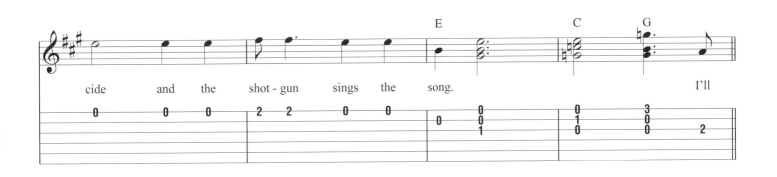

cide and the shot-gun sings the song. I'll

Chorus

tip my hat to the new con-sti-tu-tion, take a bow for the new rev-o-lu-tion.

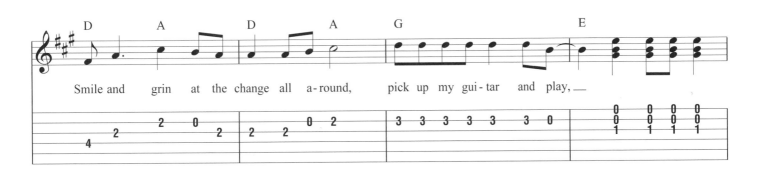

Smile and grin at the change all a-round, pick up my gui-tar and play, ____

just like yes - ter - day, ___ then I'll get on my knees and pray

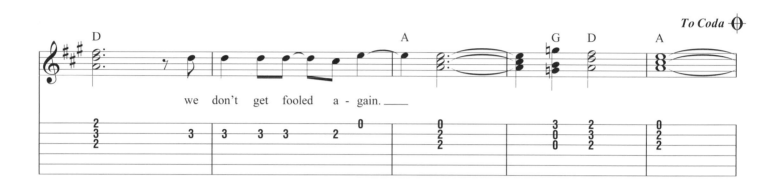

To Coda ⊕

we don't get fooled a - gain. ___

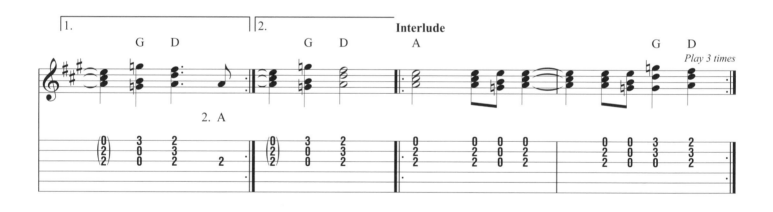

Interlude

Play 3 times

Bridge

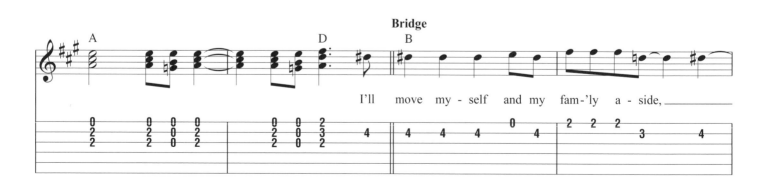

I'll move my - self and my fam - 'ly a - side, ___

if we hap-pen to be left half__ a - live.__ I'll get all my pap - ers and smile__

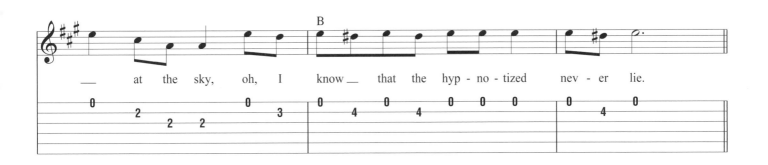

__ at the sky, oh, I know __ that the hyp - no - tized nev - er lie.

Interlude

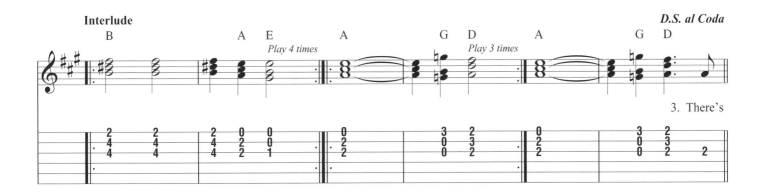

Play 4 times   *Play 3 times*   *D.S. al Coda*

3. There's

Coda

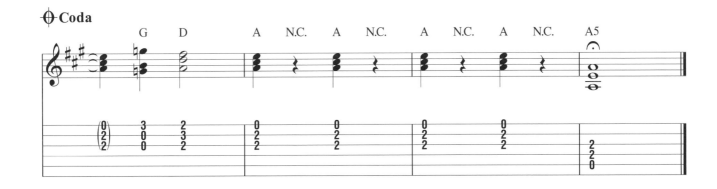

Additional Lyrics

2. A change, it had to come.
   We knew it all along.
   We were liberated from the fold, that's all.
   And the world looks just the same,
   And history ain't changed,
   'Cause the banners, they are flown in the last war.

3. There's nothing in the street
   Looks any different to me,
   And the slogans are replaced by the by.
   And the parting on the left
   Is now parting on the right,
   And the beards have all grown longer overnight.

You Better You Bet

Words and Music by Peter Townshend

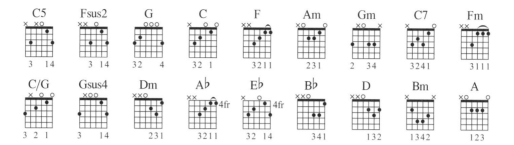

Strum Pattern: 1, 6
Pick Pattern: 5

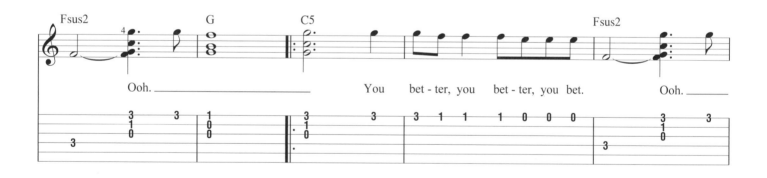

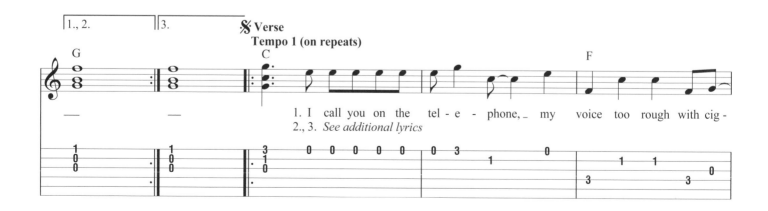

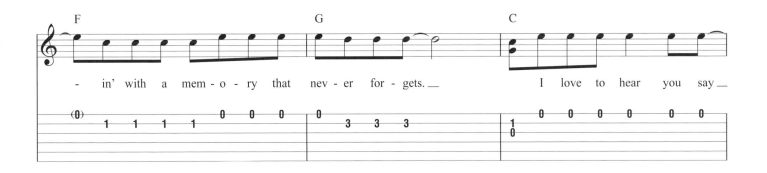

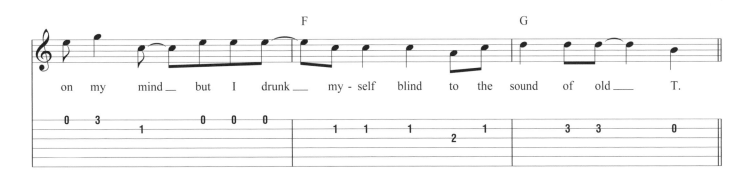

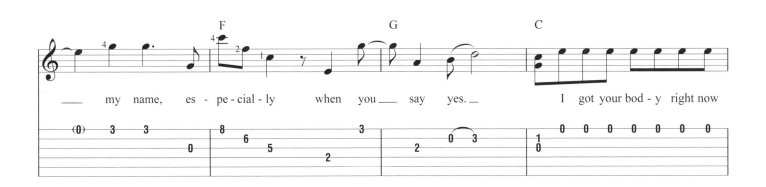

Pre-Chorus
Half-time feel

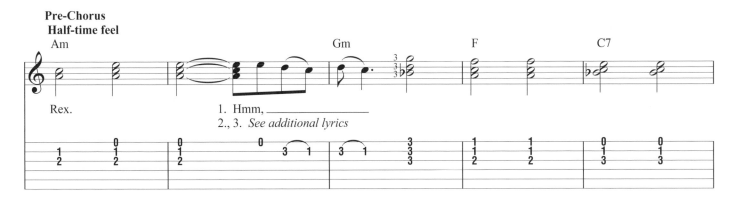

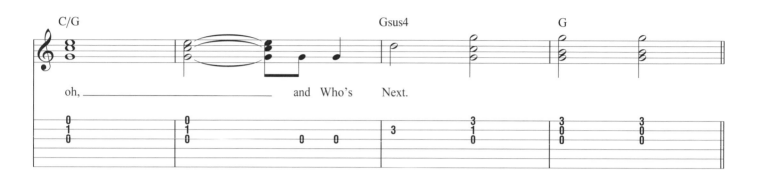

Chorus
End half-time feel

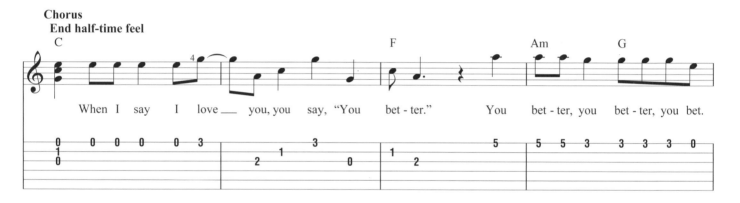

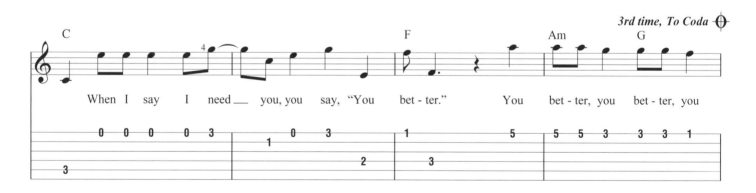

Half-time feel

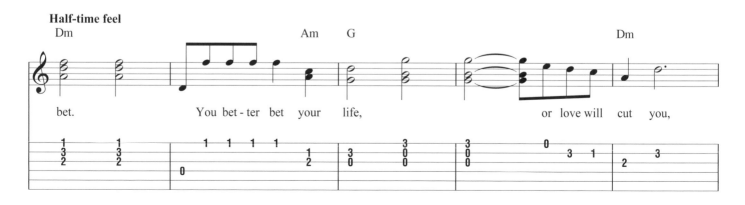

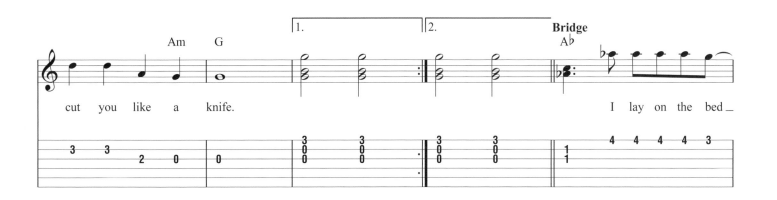

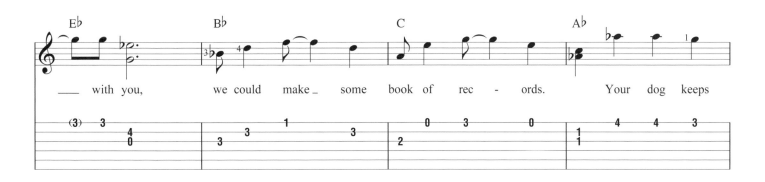

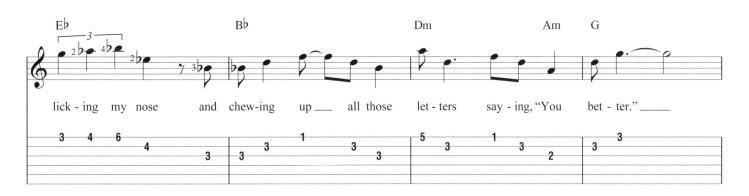

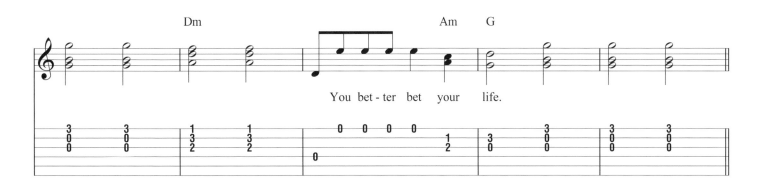

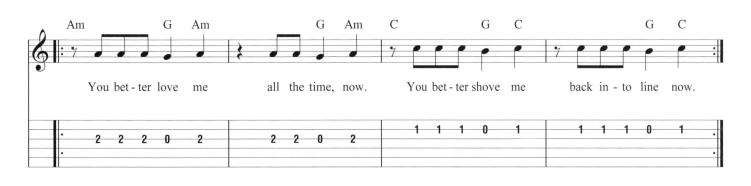

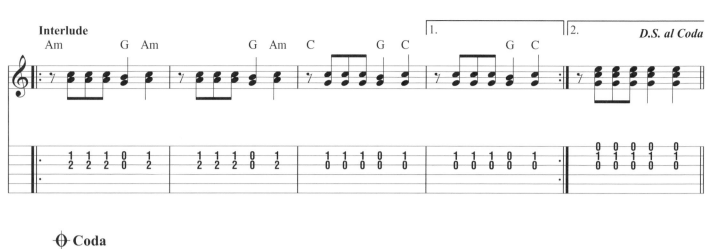

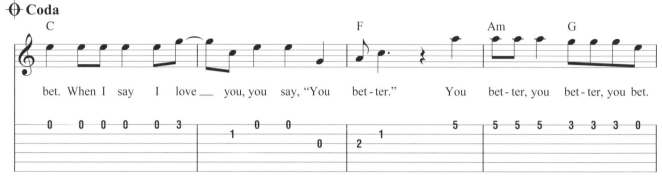

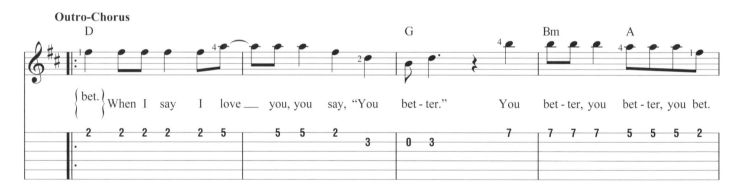

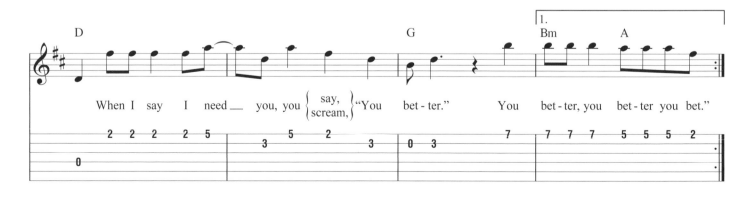

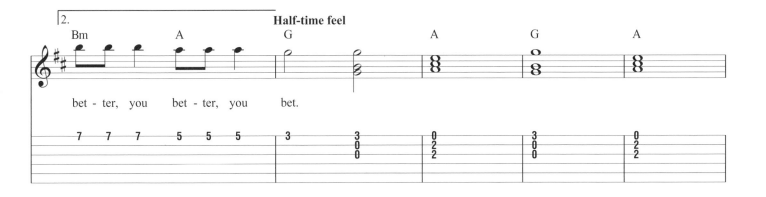

bet - ter, you   bet - ter, you   bet.

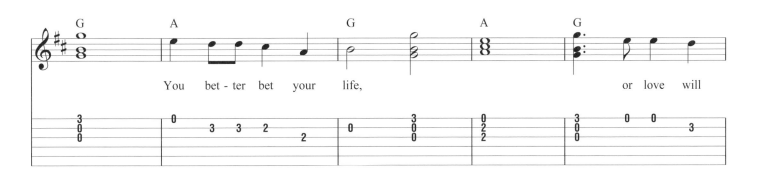

You   bet - ter bet your   life,   or   love   will

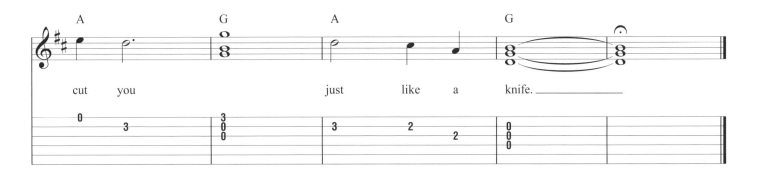

cut   you   just   like   a   knife. _____

Additional Lyrics

2. I want those feeble-minded axes overthrown.
   I'm not into your passport picture, I just like your nose.
   You welcome me with open arms and open legs.
   I know only fools have needs, but this one never begs.

Pre-Chorus 2. I don't really mind how much you love me.
   Ooh, a little is alright
   When you say, "Come over and spend the night."
   Tonight, tonight.

3. I showed up late one night with a neon light for a visa.
   But knowing I'm so eager to fight can't make letting me in any easier.
   I know I been wearin' crazy clothes and I look pretty crappy sometimes,
   But my body feels so good and I still sing a razor line every time.

Pre-Chorus 3. And when it comes to all night living,
   I know what I'm giving.
   I've got it all down to a tee.
   And it's free.

Who Are You

Words and Music by Peter Townshend

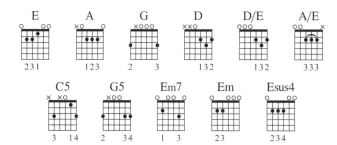

Strum Pattern: 1
Pick Pattern: 3

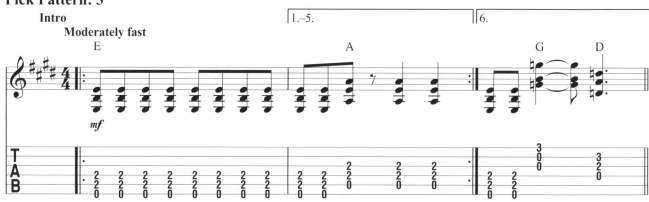

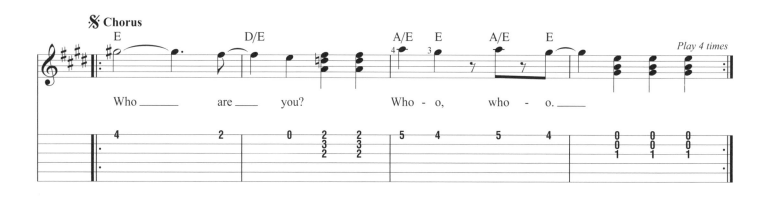

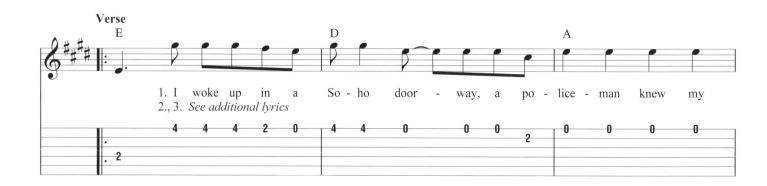

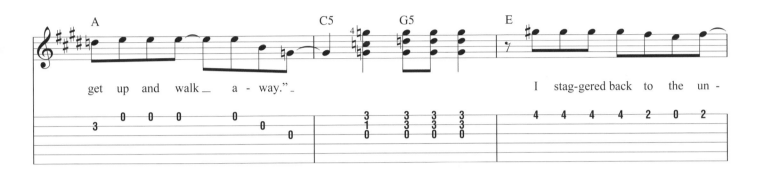

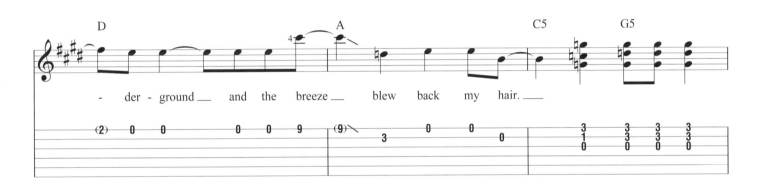

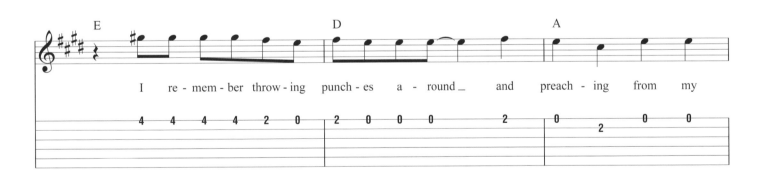

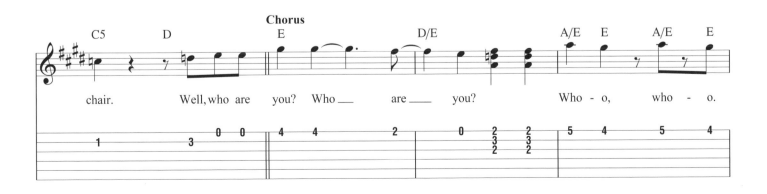

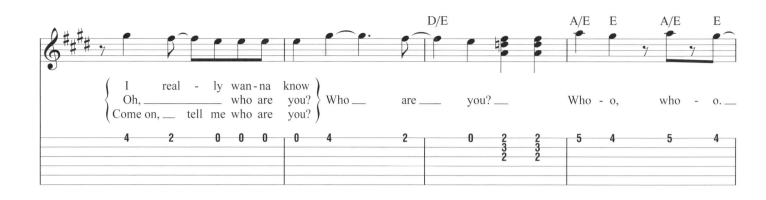

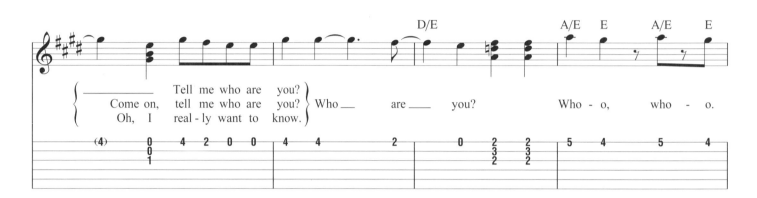

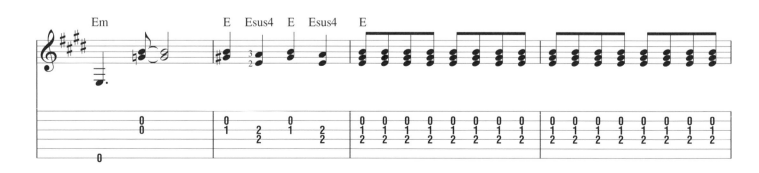

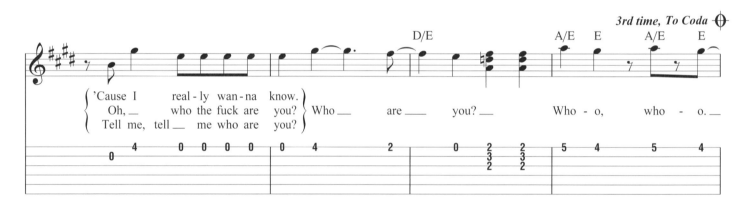

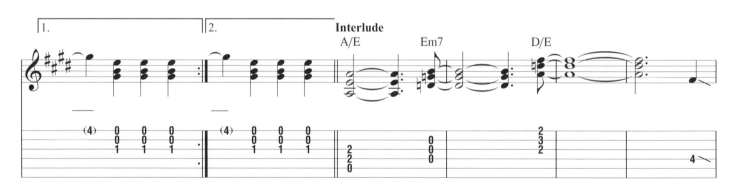

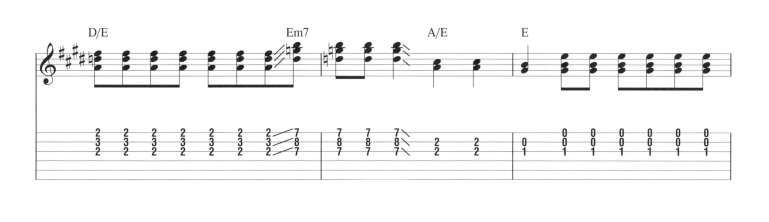

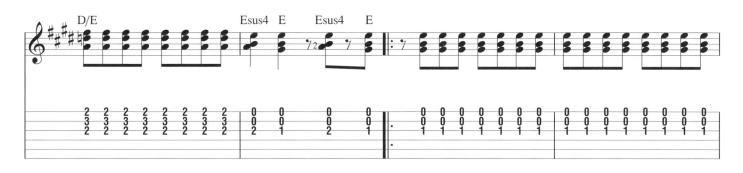

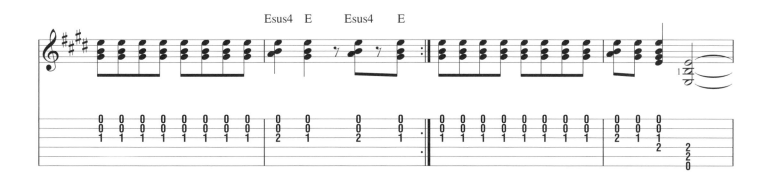

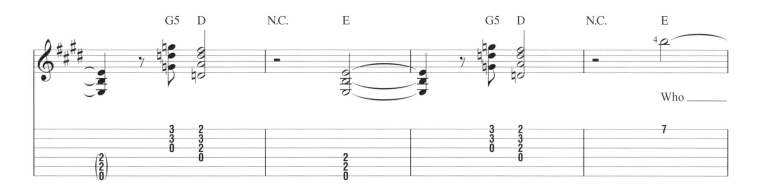

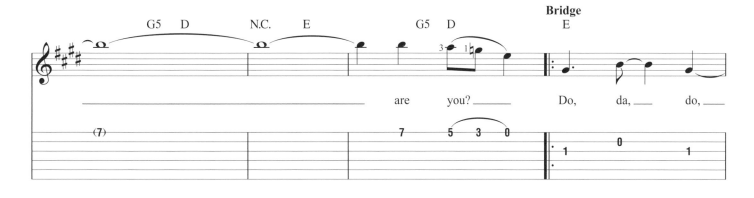

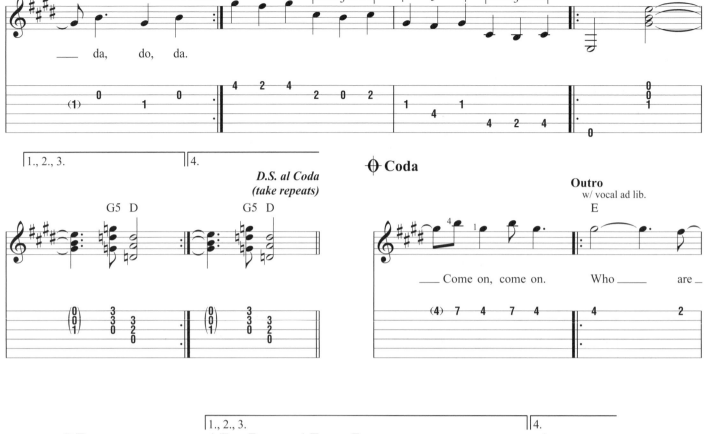

da,   do,   da.

D.S. al Coda
(take repeats)

Ⓞ **Coda**

Outro
w/ vocal ad lib.

___ Come on, come on.   Who ___   are ___

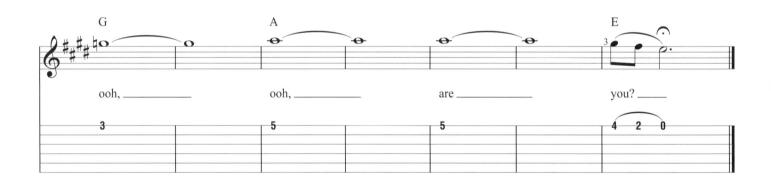

___ you?   Who - o,   who - o. ___   Who, ___

ooh, ___   ooh, ___   are ___   you? ___

Additional Lyrics

2. I took the tube back out of town, back to the Rollin' Pin.
    I felt a little like a dying hound with a streak of "Rin Tin Tin."
    I stretched back and I hiccupped, and looked back on my busy day.
    Eleven hours in the tin pan, God, there's got to be another way.

3. I know there's a place you walked where love falls from the trees.
    My heart is like a broken cup, I only feel right on my knees.
    I spill out like a sewer hole and still receive your kiss.
    How can I measure up to anyone now, after such a love as this?